Dips

~

Great Recipes for Spreads, Salsas, Fondues and Other Party Fare

SUSAN PUCKETT

LONGSTREET PRESS, INC.
Atlanta, Georgia

Published by LONGSTREET PRESS, INC.,
a subsidiary of Cox Newspapers,
a subsidiary of Cox Enterprises, Inc.
2140 Newmarket Parkway
Suite 118
Marietta, Georgia 30067

Printed in the United States

1st printing, 1995

Library of Congress Catalog Number 95-77254

ISBN: 1-56352-241-1

Jacket and book design by Jill Dible

Photography by Al Clayton, Atlanta, Georgia
Food styling by Mary Ann Clayton, Atlanta, Georgia

Electronic film prep and separations by Advertising Technologies, Inc., Atlanta, GA

Table of Contents

~

Introduction

My friend Beth is not shy when it comes to trying out new recipes on friends. She rolls her own sushi. She spins sugar to decorate cakes. And she serves California Dip with pride — at virtually every party she throws or attends which requires an offering.

"That's my litmus test to see how well people really like my other experiments," she says. "If the dip is only half-eaten, then I know they must be a success. If it's demolished, then chances are the other stuff hasn't been touched."

But never does the lumpy, beige mixture get ignored, no matter how elaborate its competition.

Americans have been devouring "Festive California Dip" by the shovelful since the recipe first appeared on the back of the box of Lipton's dehydrated onion soup mix in 1954. The recipe could not have been simpler: Stir package contents into a bowl of sour cream. Tear open a potato chip bag. Set out on the boomerang table. Add guests, Patti Page's latest record, and get dipping!

It was the instant hors d'oeuvre millions of new suburbanites, weary of soggy canapés and messy cocktail meatballs, were looking for. They loved its devilishly rich, salty taste. They loved even more its preparation time, which barely exceeded the seconds it took to open and close the refrigerator door.

Soup mix sales soared. Sour cream sales, too. Special chip-and-dip trays turned up at bridal showers everywhere, along with fondue pots, which became a sensation in 1956. Mayonnaise, cream cheese, Velveeta and similarly bland, creamy substances were transformed into chipped beef dip and clam dip and hot queso dip on party trays and in chafing dishes across the country. Hosts and hostesses devised their own clever combinations and swapped recipes with family and friends.

Not everyone welcomed this breakthrough in home entertainment.

"Down, down to hell itself . . . with dips," decreed the renowned food writer M. F. K. Fisher in *With Bold Knife and Fork*. "The idea of all kinds of wafers and chips and plastic skewers dabbling in a common bowl, and often breaking off in it, [is] repugnant."

She did have one legitimate beef about dips: the chipped-chip dilemma. This was not lost on snack food manufacturers. In the quest for a scoop sturdy enough to withstand the weight of these glorious glops, a corrugated delivery system was invented:

The ridged potato chip. Today there is an endless grocery aisle of chips and crackers from which to choose — most designed with dip resistance in mind.

This engineering advance probably did little to sway M. F. K.'s thinking on the subject, although sometimes I do wonder if, left alone in a room with nothing but a bowl of dip and bag of chips, she really would have been able to eat just one.

But even gastronomes who wouldn't touch a bowl of such unabashedly unrefined stuff with a ten-foot bread stick likely wouldn't hesitate to dive right into a freshly made cilantro-spiked tomatillo salsa with a blue corn chip, cumin-scented Middle Eastern hummus with a pita triangle, the Italian anchovy sauce known as bagna cauda with a Belgian endive leaf. In fact, M. F. K. herself has admitted to dipping from communal bowls of guacamole, caviar pie, pâté, brandied chopped liver — and enjoying it! These international classics, too, are technically dips — even though they were fortunate enough to have been created long before that dippy term.

While I was gathering recipes for this book and picking the brains of the great cooks I know for suggestions, one friend implied to me that dips were now passé. "I haven't dipped in *years*," she sniffed.

My suspicion, though, is that she and many other foodies like her are in dip denial. At other people's parties, they glare at the dip bowl in disdain, and then plunge in while no one is watching. At their own parties, they even serve them, but under pseudonyms like "pâté" and "mousse" and, as one famous trendy cookbook author has called them, "slather."

Rare is the occasion that I've been to — whether it be an elegant champagne wedding reception or a B.Y.O.B. Super Bowl party — that at least a few dips aren't present. After all, just about everyone loves them, they require no utensils, their communal nature invites conviviality, and who has the time nowadays to assemble hundreds of fussy little hors d'oeuvres anyway?

For the time-pressed cook, a great dip is the perfect potluck offering: More thoughtful and impressive than store-bought or take-out, yet just about as easy. Dips also satisfy our growing grazing instincts. Provided they're not too fatty — and many of the recipes in this book are not — they can make a satisfying little meal, or part of a meal.

That familiar onion-soup-mix-and-sour-cream concoction still has a standing invitation at many gatherings — why else would the recipe still be on the package? — as do a handful of other newer favorites that seem to have wound up in everyone's file box: layered bean dip, hot artichoke dip, ranch dressing in a hollowed-out cabbage, to name a few.

There's something comforting about those enduring favorites, but as reliable as they are, they can get monotonous.

In a quest for some more imaginative options, the *Atlanta Journal-Constitution*, of which I am food editor, recently had a contest asking readers for dip recipes. We encouraged them to think new. No moldy oldies need apply. Some 500 responses poured in — far more good ones than the paper had space to run. Shortly after we ran our results, my fellow food editor at the *Palm Beach Post*, Jan Norris, conducted a similar contest in her food pages with an equal show of enthusiasm.

Obviously, a lot of folks were into dipping. But it occurred to me that I'd never seen a collection of great dips in one volume. That's how this book came to be. Along with the best recipes from these two contests, I began collecting and testing recipes from home cooks, caterers and other food professionals in Atlanta and elsewhere. For months, volunteer testers and tasters would take turns hosting a "dipathon" in their homes. We tried to get as creative with the dippers as the dips themselves, pairing polenta chips with a roasted red pepper dip, Romaine lettuce leaves and Parmesan croutons with a Caesar dip, wonton bow ties with an Asian soy-sesame dip, crunchy miniature meringues with a crème anglaise dessert dip.

I allowed dips' spreadable siblings into the mix — pâtés, mousses, cheese crocks — as well as fondues, salsas and basically any sauce or spread that could be eaten without utensils.

In this book you will find dips and spreads for every mood and occasion — both innovative and tried-and-true classics. There are hot dips and cold dips, savory dips and sweet dips, fancy dips and casual dips, exotic dips and familiar dips. While some of the recipes are more challenging than others, they're all relatively easy — some, in fact, have only two or three ingredients. We've also devoted an entire chapter to "skinny dips," which includes salsas and other dips that taste great, but just happen to be low in fat. But now that mayonnaise, sour cream and cream cheese have their fat-reduced and fat-free counterparts, most of the recipes in this book could be made "skinny" quite easily.

So you see, there is more to dips than sour cream and pre-fab soup mix — a lot more. Come into my kitchen and I'll show you.

Dip Tips

Let's be honest: It doesn't take much creativity to make a great-tasting dip; for the most part, you simply toss the ingredients into a mixing bowl or food processor, give it a whirl and serve.

But you can go to town on the presentation. Break out of the carrot-and-celery stick rut and open your mind to some less predictable crudité platter combinations. Try some new vegetables you may have overlooked. Two that come to mind are jicama, the homely brown Mexican tuber; and kohlrabi, the green-skinned turnip cousin. Peel away the skins and in both you'll find a crisp, sweet, white flesh that is made for cutting into sticks and eating raw or, better yet, dunking in some flavorful dip.

Though the word "crudités" technically refers to raw vegetables, a crudité platter need not be restricted to such. Some vegetables taste better and look prettier if they are cooked or blanched quickly first (instructions follow). Nor do crudité platters need to be exclusive. Skewered meats, fruits and stuffed pastas are often welcome, depending on the dip.

To carry out the crudité theme, consider hollowing out a cabbage or other vegetable to use as a dip bowl (other suggestions follow).

For each recipe, I'll offer suggestions for dippers, but don't be limited to those. Here are some ideas to get you to thinking of your own.

VEGETABLE DIPPERS

Raw vegetables:

Bell peppers (green, red, yellow, purple)
Celery sticks, stalks with tops
Cherry or plum tomatoes
Cucumber slices, spears
Belgian endive leaves
Fennel slices, sticks
Scallions
Jicama slices, sticks
Kohlrabi slices
Turnip spears, slices
Whole mushrooms
Romaine lettuce leaves (firm inner
  leaves)
Raddiccio leaves
Whole red and white radishes
Yellow squash slices, spears or sticks
Zucchini slices, spears or sticks

Clockwise, from top: Roasted Yellow Pepper Dip;
Five-Pepper Pesto; Smoky Red Pepper Dip; Goat
Cheese Dip with Bell Pepper and Chives

Blanched vegetables:

Asparagus
Broccoli
Broccoflower
Brussels sprouts
Carrots (whole baby carrots, carrot
  sticks, carrot curls)
Cauliflower
Green beans
Snow peas
Sugar snaps

Cooked/canned/bottled vegetables:

Artichokes (fresh leaves; canned hearts,
  bottoms; whole baby artichokes)
Beets (cooked or canned, drained and
  blotted dry)
New potatoes
Potato skins
Canned baby corn
Pickled green beans
Pickled mushrooms
Gherkins, cornichons

SKEWERED DIPPERS

Cooked tortellini or ravioli
Grilled chicken tenders or nuggets
Cooked jumbo shrimp or bay scallops
Steak strips
Pepperoni, salami or other cold cut slices

Kielbasa slices
Smoked ham or turkey cubes

CHIPS, CRACKERS, BREADS

Ritz and other butter-flavored crackers
Potato chips
Corn chips
Bagel chips
Tortilla chips — flour, corn, blue corn
Pretzels, pretzel chips
Plain and sesame bread sticks
Water biscuits
Champagne biscuits
Bremner wafers
Pita bread, chips
French bread, baguette rounds
Rye, pumpernickel party rounds and
  crackers
Lahvosh
Matzo
Melba toast
Holland rusks
Wasa bread
Zwieback toast
Shrimp and crab-flavored chips
  (available in Asian markets)
Pappadams (Indian flat bread; available
  in Indian markets)

FRUITS

Apple slices, chunks
Banana chunks
Pineapple chunks
Melon balls
Carambola (star fruit) slices
Cherries
Blueberries
Blackberries
Strawberries
Grapes
Pear slices
Mango slices, chunks
Papaya slices, chunks
Fresh coconut chunks
Orange, mandarin orange sections

SWEET DIPPERS

Pound cake
Angel food cake
Graham crackers
Vanilla wafers
Chocolate wafers
Brownie chunks
Meringues
Oreos
Coconut macaroons
Butter cookies
Marshmallows
Small, plain doughnuts
Ladyfingers

EDIBLE DIP CONTAINERS

Using a sharp knife, hollow out and drain well, if necessary:

Purple or green cabbage
Colored bell peppers
Winter squash, pattypan squash
Pumpkins
Pineapple halves
Melons
Round loaves of pumpernickel, sour-
   dough or other crusty bread

PRESENTATION

Here are some suggestions for preparing and displaying fruits and vegetables:

Choosing: Be flexible. If only fat, woody asparagus spears are available, bypass them in favor of beautiful peak-season broccoli, or whatever else happens to look the freshest, brightest and crispest.

Trimming: Peel vegetables and fruits if necessary, then cut neatly and uniformly to make convenient-sized finger foods. Cut them up early in the day, but no more than 8 hours in advance.

Blanching: You can enhance the taste, color and texture of many vegetables that are intended for dipping by blanching them first. This means that they are quickly immersed into boiling water just until they're crisp-tender. Blanching time depends on the size and tenderness of the vegetable; snow peas or sugar snaps could take less than a minute; carrots or Brussels sprouts could take more than five minutes. Watch them closely and drain as soon as their color turns bright and they are crisp-tender when pierced in the thickest part with a fork. Drain the vegetables in a colander, then either run cold water over them to prevent further cooking, or — better yet — plunge them in a bowl of ice water.

Storing: When cool, store the prepped vegetables separately in plastic containers of ice water — unless their texture and flavor will be destroyed by a water bath, such as potatoes, tomatoes, avocados or anything pickled or marinated. Cover and refrigerate until you're ready to arrange the platter.
Spread out cut-up fruits on separate baking trays, cover with damp paper towels, wrap tightly in plastic wrap and refrigerate until just before serving time.

ARRANGING DIP AND CRUDITÉ PLATTERS

Choosing containers: You don't need an arsenal of fancy serving platters to serve crudités and dips with style. You can create striking displays atop a wooden cutting board or pastry marble, in a wicker basket or heart-shaped cake pan, or on a TV tray or framed mirror. You could also stand the vegetables upright and group them in crystal or glass wine goblets and place at individual settings.

Designing a platter: Keep the platter designs simple. To keep edges straight between sections, lay the edge of a piece of cardboard or the side of a spatula where you want each section to end. Slide out your guide when the food is in place.

Tip: If you're using an upright basket, pad the base with crumpled wax paper to raise the display. Also, put the stick-vegetables into the basket vertically and arrange other cut vegetables in neat piles, fanning out the top layer.

Designing with color: Stick to no more than three or four colors to avoid a busy appearance. Place contrasting colors next to each other (green beans next to cherry tomatoes, for example) to intensify the colors of each. For a subtler effect, juxtapose colors that are next to each other on the color wheel (consider red, orange and yellow pepper strips). A monochromatic pattern can also be striking: Arrange different shades of the same color from light to dark — Belgian endive leaves, celery, green beans, broccoli.

Final touches: Some fruits and vegetables — apples, pears, peaches — turn brown after they've been cut. Squeezing lemon juice over them will help prevent discoloration. Or, set them in a bowl of water mixed with a little lemon juice for a few minutes after cutting. But don't go sprinkling lemon juice on everything thinking that it will brighten their color. Lemon juice, vinegar and other acidic ingredients can turn green vegetables such as green beans and broccoli a sickly yellow color. Adding a little baking soda to the blanching water can crank up the color a notch or two, but it can also damage the B-vitamin content; you decide if it's worth it.

TOOLS

A good, sharp knife is really the only tool you need to make pretty crudités, but if you want to add a fancier edge or shape to a vegetable or fruit, kitchenware shops can supply you with the tools you need:

Fluting knife: Also known as a corrugated cutter, this knife has a ridged blade that cuts vegetables and fruit into slices resembling corrugated cardboard. It works best with firm-fleshed vegetables and fruits such as carrots, beets, turnips and apples.

Citrus zester: This tool strips into thin slivers the zest (colored outer skin, above the spongy white pith) of citrus fruits. It also can be used for other fruits and to make designs in the skin of vegetables. If you score a grooved pattern into the skin of a fruit or vegetable — cucumbers, say — and then slice it, you'll get an interesting "striped" skin.

Wedge knife: This knife creates uniform zigzag edges on the edges of melons such as cantaloupe, honeydew and watermelon. The fruit can then be scooped out and the shell used for an attractive dip container.

Melon ball cutters: These tools are available in a wide range of sizes and types, such as fluted and oval shapes. The standard round cutter and its counterparts can be used to make balls from the flesh of fruits and vegetables.

Cookie cutters: They're not just for dough: Use them also to cut shapes from flat slices of fruit such as pineapple or watermelon.

Mandoline: This slicing tool can make slices, weaves, crinkle cuts and julienne strips of firm vegetables such as potatoes and carrots in varying thicknesses. It also shreds cabbage well, is faster to use than a knife and is generally more exact than a food processor.

HOST YOUR OWN "DIPATHON"

Dipping is a fun, easy way to entertain your friends; in fact, you can build a whole party around dips — I got pretty good at it while testing the recipes for this book. Here are a few thoughts for hosting your own dipathon:

1. Offer dips with a variety of flavors and textures, and make sure you don't go too heavy on the fatty mayonnaise and cream cheese-based ones. Include a salsa or two, for instance.

2. Vary the dippers. Make sure that besides chips, you've got a nice selection of crudités. A few more substantial dippers, such as grilled meats or stuffed pasta on skewers, are also welcome.

3. Make the dips at least several hours ahead to blend flavors. Most are actually better the next day. (Fondues are an exception.)

4. Don't stick yourself with all the work. It's not an inconvenience for most people to come up with a dip. So make it a potluck.

Whether you're throwing a dipathon or attending one, don't forget your dip etiquette:

▲ Use edible dippers only. Fingers are not acceptable — except for chicken fingers, maybe.

▲ Rescue broken chips and other drowned dippers with a spoon, not your fingers.

▲ Don't hog the dip bowl. Fix a plate and move on.

▲ Beware of drippy dips. It's a good idea to make sure there's a paper plate or a napkin between you and the carpet.

▲ And don't even think about double-dipping — that is, dipping into the community dip bowl, taking a bite, then dipping again. As George on a "Seinfeld" episode was told, "Take one dip and end it!"

Garden Dips

~

Dips haven't always been paired with fresh produce; the earlier ones were almost always chemical-laden concoctions designed to perch atop a potato chip or a cracker. Then in the 1970s, we started crunching on raw veggies because it was the natural thing to do. Carrot and celery sticks were sturdy enough to scoop up many of the good old familiar dips. But we also started experimenting with fresher formulas that drew their flavor from herbs and minced vegetables. Into them we dipped crudités inspired by new discoveries in the produce bin: sugar snaps, baby squash, jicama sticks.

I associate the dips in this chapter with the late spring and summer months when most produce is at its peak. Several are salads made dippable: potato salad, Greek salad, salade niçoise. They are particularly well-suited for patio parties, bridal showers and picnics in the park. Some dips that rely heavily on vegetables as a lowfat base can be found in the "Skinny Dips" chapter; look for traditional salsa and other ethnic blends in the "Worldly Dips" chapter.

Fresh Lemon-Basil Dip

Fresh Lemon-Basil Dip

~

MAKES 1 1/4 CUPS / PREPARATION TIME: 15 MINUTES

Skewered, cooked tortellini, boiled shrimp, lightly blanched asparagus or cooked artichoke leaves are just right for dipping into this smooth, summery sauce. Or spoon over steamed vegetables and poached or smoked salmon.

1/4 cup fresh lemon juice
1 teaspoon sugar
1/2 cup fresh basil leaves
1/2 teaspoon salt
1/4 cup fresh parsley leaves
1 clove garlic, chopped
1 cup mayonnaise

In a blender or food processor, combine all ingredients except mayonnaise. Process until smooth. In a medium bowl, whip mayonnaise until creamy. Stir in herb mixture. Cover and refrigerate until ready to serve.

Carrot-Raisin Dip

~

MAKES 1 1/2 CUPS / PREPARATION TIME: 10 MINUTES

Not just for dipping, this nutty-sweet mixture is great for filling celery stalks or spreading in sandwiches.

> 8 ounces cream cheese, softened
> 1/2 cup grated carrots
> 1/4 cup raisins
> 1/4 cup pecan pieces
> salt to taste
> carrot curls, parsley sprigs for garnish
>   (optional)

In a medium bowl, beat cream cheese until smooth. In a food processor, finely chop carrots, raisins and pecans. Stir mixture into cream cheese. Add salt. Cover and refrigerate until ready to serve. Garnish with carrot curls or parsley sprigs. Or, decorate with an already peeled and cleaned baby carrot to which you have added a parsley sprig for the top.

Goat Cheese Dip
with Bell Pepper and Chives

~

MAKES ABOUT 2 CUPS / PREPARATION TIME: 15 MINUTES

At the Television Food Network in New York, guests aren't sent to the vending machines to get rid of stomach butterflies. They are led to the "green room" for primping, and nibbling on whatever surprises the kitchen staff has set out. While waiting to go on the air to talk about barbecue sauce, I got so carried away dipping pita chips into this creamy, chive-flecked spread I almost forgot my spiel. After the show, I tracked down its creator, who laughed when I asked her for the recipe. "We mixed that up while we were cleaning out the refrigerator," said Lynn Kearney, a freelance chef and food stylist whose job is making food look pretty before the cameras. This recipe proves she can make it taste great, too.

Besides pita chips, it suits raw and blanched vegetables of all kinds, especially snow peas, baby carrots, radishes and bell pepper strips.

3 3 1/2-ounce packages goat cheese
3/4 cup sour cream
2 to 4 tablespoons minced green, red or yellow bell pepper (or a combination)
2 tablespoons minced chives
1 clove garlic, finely minced
1 teaspoon lemon juice
salt and freshly ground black pepper to taste
extra virgin olive oil (optional)
snipped chives for garnish (optional)

In a medium nonreactive bowl, with an electric mixer, blend the goat cheese and sour cream until smooth. Stir in the bell pepper, chives, garlic and lemon juice. Add salt and pepper. Cover and refrigerate until ready to serve. Transfer to a serving platter or bowl. If desired, drizzle with olive oil and garnish with chives.

Vampire Vaccine

~

MAKES ABOUT 1 1/4 CUPS / PREPARATION TIME: 45 MINUTES
CHILLING TIME: OVERNIGHT / STANDING TIME: 1 HOUR

No need to worry about some uninvited vampire showing up on your doorstep when you serve this potion. Actually, the flavor is not as sharp as you might imagine — when baked, the garlic mellows and softens to a buttery consistency. Dunk in with pita chips, boiled potatoes, broccoli spears and most any sturdy vegetable.

2 bulbs (about 30 cloves) garlic, separated
1 tablespoon olive oil
8 ounces cream cheese, softened
1 tablespoon mayonnaise
1 teaspoon lemon juice
1/2 teaspoon soy sauce
salt to taste
5 to 6 drops hot pepper sauce
1 tablespoon chopped chives

Preheat oven to 325 degrees. Blanch garlic cloves in a small pot of boiling water. Run cold water over them, then remove and discard the skins. (They should come off easily by pinching a clove between your thumb and forefinger, or press with the flat side of a knife.) Arrange cloves in a baking dish in a single layer. Toss with olive oil until coated. Bake for 20 to 30 minutes, or until very soft. Remove from oven and cool. In a food processor, puree garlic. Add remaining ingredients except chives. Process until smooth. Transfer to a serving bowl. Stir in chives. Cover and refrigerate overnight. Let stand at room temperature for 1 hour before serving.

Tomato-Feta Dip

~

MAKES 3 CUPS / PREPARATION TIME: 10 MINUTES
CHILLING TIME: 1 HOUR

If you're a Greek salad fan, you'll love this pleasantly pungent dip, which can be scooped up with pita triangles, cucumbers or Romaine lettuce leaves.

2 medium tomatoes
8 ounces feta cheese
3 tablespoons olive oil
3 cloves garlic, minced
2 scallions, chopped
1 tablespoon fresh oregano leaves, or 1 teaspoon dried
10 cured black Greek olives, pitted
cured black Greek olives, fresh oregano leaves for garnish
  (optional)

Fill a medium saucepan with water and bring to a boil. Drop whole tomatoes in and cook for 10 seconds. When cool enough to handle, peel off skin. Chop tomatoes into large chunks and drain excess liquid. In a food processor, combine tomatoes, cheese, olive oil, garlic, scallions, oregano and olives. Process until smooth. Transfer to a serving bowl. Refrigerate for 1 hour before serving. Garnish with olives and oregano leaves.

Niçoise Dip

~

MAKES 2 CUPS / PREPARATION TIME: 10 MINUTES

This robust dip draws its inspiration from the South of France. Use the ingredients of classic salade niçoise as dippers: blanched green beans, boiled new potatoes, cherry tomatoes, small lettuce leaves.

2 cloves garlic, peeled
1 6-ounce can tuna, drained
1/2 cup mayonnaise
2 tablespoons Dijon mustard
4 anchovies
4 scallions, chopped
1/2 teaspoon ground white pepper
2 teaspoons lemon juice
1 tablespoon capers
black olives, chopped hard-boiled egg for garnish
*   (optional)*

In a food processor, with motor running, drop garlic cloves through the chute. Process until minced. Add tuna, mayonnaise, mustard, anchovies, scallions, white pepper and lemon juice. Process until smooth. Fold in capers. Transfer to a serving bowl. Cover and refrigerate until ready to serve. Garnish with olives and egg.

Potato Salad Dip

~

MAKES 4 CUPS / PREPARATION TIME: 45 MINUTES
CHILLING TIME: 2 TO 3 HOURS

Instead of a fork, use a potato chip or a bell pepper wedge to scoop up this extra-creamy version of the picnic classic.

1 pound Yukon gold or other potatoes, peeled and cut in
  1-inch cubes (about 3 1/2 cups)
2/3 cup plain yogurt
1/3 cup mayonnaise
1/2 cup finely chopped Vidalia or other sweet onion
1/3 cup finely diced celery
1 tablespoon finely chopped parsley
1/3 cup sweet pickle relish
1 hard-boiled egg, chopped
parsley, chopped boiled egg, paprika for garnish (optional)

In a large pan, cover potatoes with water. Bring to a boil. Lower the heat and simmer until tender, about 15 to 20 minutes. Drain potatoes. Transfer to a large bowl. With an electric mixer, beat on low speed to break up the potatoes. Add yogurt and mayonnaise. Beat until smooth. Transfer to a medium bowl. Stir in the remaining ingredients. Cover and refrigerate for 2 to 3 hours before serving. Garnish with parsley, egg and paprika.

Deviled Egg Dip with Herbs

~

MAKES 1 1/2 CUPS / PREPARATION TIME: 15 MINUTES

Deviled eggs are a bit tedious to assemble — so don't. Mix all those flavors together and dip into it with celery, carrot strips and wheat crackers.

> *3 ounces cream cheese, softened*
> *1/4 cup mayonnaise*
> *1 tablespoon milk*
> *5 hard-boiled eggs, chopped*
> *1 tablespoon mustard*
> *1/4 teaspoon onion salt*
> *ground white or black pepper to taste*
> *2 teaspoons chopped dill (or 1/2 teaspoon dried)*
> *2 teaspoons chopped chives (or 1/2 teaspoon dried)*
> *1 teaspoon horseradish, or to taste (optional)*
> *paprika for garnish (optional)*

In a medium bowl, with an electric mixer, beat the cream cheese, mayonnaise and milk until smooth. Stir in remaining ingredients. Cover and refrigerate until ready to serve. Garnish with paprika.

Five-Pepper Pesto

MAKES 1 1/2 CUPS / PREPARATION TIME: 25 MINUTES

Peppers both sweet and hot are the basis for these two dips. Cilantro and lime temper pale-green Five-Pepper Pesto; Smoky Red Pepper Dip gets its smoky-hot taste from canned chipotles: smoked jalapeño peppers packed in a spicy adobo sauce. Served side by side, surrounded by white and blue corn tortilla chips, their contrasting colors make a striking presentation.

1/2 yellow bell pepper, stemmed, seeded and chopped
1 jalapeño pepper, stemmed, seeded and chopped
2 poblano peppers, stemmed, seeded and chopped
3 Anaheim peppers, stemmed, seeded and chopped
1/2 teaspoon black pepper
3 cloves garlic, chopped
1/3 cup chopped parsley
1 tablespoon chopped cilantro
1/2 cup pine nuts
2 ounces feta cheese, crumbled (1/2 cup)
1 tablespoon lime juice
1/2 cup olive oil
salt to taste
parsley or cilantro for garnish (optional)

In a food processor, combine all ingredients except olive oil, salt and garnish. With the machine running, gradually add olive oil to make a thick, smooth paste. Transfer mixture to a serving bowl. Salt to taste. Cover and refrigerate until ready to serve. Let stand for 30 minutes before serving. Garnish with parsley or cilantro.

Smoky Red Pepper Dip

~

MAKES 2 CUPS / PREPARATION TIME: 45 MINUTES
STANDING TIME: 1 HOUR

For an intriguing dipper, make *Polenta Chips:* Buy a roll of prepared polenta and slice thinly, then place on a lightly oiled baking sheet. Broil about 4 inches from heat source for about 20 minutes, flipping once halfway in between, or until polenta browns and is crisp on the edges.

2 medium red bell peppers, roasted (see note below), stemmed,
   peeled, seeded and coarsely chopped
1 ancho pepper, stemmed, seeded and coarsely chopped
1 poblano pepper, stemmed, seeded and coarsely chopped
1/2 chipotle pepper in adobo sauce
1/8 teaspoon adobo sauce from the can (or to taste)
1/2 cup shredded Monterey Jack cheese
3 tablespoons olive oil
1/4 cup light cream
1 teaspoon paprika
1/2 teaspoon salt
1/4 teaspoon brown sugar
cilantro sprigs for garnish (optional)

In a food processor, combine all ingredients except garnish. Puree until smooth. Let stand at room temperature for 1 hour before serving, to let flavors meld. Garnish with cilantro sprigs.

Note: Prick the bell peppers with a fork in several spots. On a hot grill or under a broiler, roast the peppers on all sides until skin is blackened. Drop the peppers in a paper bag, close it up and let them steam for about 15 minutes. Scrape skin from the peppers. Discard skin.

Chopped Green Bean Pâté

~

MAKES 2 1/2 CUPS / PREPARATION TIME: 30 MINUTES

This dip has been described as a low-cholesterol substitute for chopped liver. But its light, fresh, nutty flavor will appeal to liver haters, also. Spread on bagel chips or party rye.

1 tablespoon vegetable oil or nonstick vegetable spray
1 medium onion, chopped
3/4 pound green beans, cooked al dente and drained
3 hard-boiled eggs, peeled
1 cup walnuts
1/3 cup light mayonnaise
salt and black pepper to taste
dash of ground red pepper
parsley sprigs for garnish (optional)

Lightly coat a nonstick skillet with oil or spray. Over medium heat, sauté onion until golden and translucent. Transfer to a food processor. Add green beans, eggs and walnuts. Process until chopped to desired consistency. Transfer to a medium bowl. Add mayonnaise, salt and peppers. Cover and refrigerate until ready to serve. Garnish with parsley sprigs.

Radish Dip

~

MAKES ABOUT 1 1/4 CUPS / PREPARATION TIME: 15 MINUTES

Radishes and scallions add vivid color and a surprise peppery bite to this creamy dip shared by Anne Hamilton of Marietta, Georgia. In the dip recipe contest sponsored by the *Atlanta Journal-Constitution*, it took first place in a field of 500 entries. Dip in with whole radishes, scallions, carrot sticks and whole-grain crackers.

8 ounces cream cheese, softened
1/4 cup (1/2 stick) butter or margarine, softened
1/2 teaspoon celery salt
dash of paprika
1/2 teaspoon Worcestershire sauce
1 cup finely chopped radishes
1/4 cup finely chopped scallions
radish rose for garnish (optional)

In a medium bowl, with an electric mixer, blend cream cheese, butter, celery salt, paprika and Worcestershire sauce. Fold in radishes and scallions. Cover and refrigerate until ready to serve. Garnish with radish rose.

To make a radish rose: cut through the center of the radish lengthwise almost to the green top, without cutting through. Make two equal cuts on each side of the center cut. Make identical perpendicular cuts. Hold the radish in ice water for 1 to 2 hours until "petals" open. Arrange the radish flower on an herb sprig (parsley, mint, etc.) to resemble a stem.

Confetti Dip

~

This sprightly, sweet and sour dip is good with both vegetables and fruits — particularly bell peppers, carrots and apples.

3 eggs, beaten
3 tablespoons sugar
3 tablespoons cider vinegar
1 teaspoon butter
8 ounces cream cheese, softened
dash of hot pepper sauce
2 tablespoons grated onion
1/2 green bell pepper, stemmed, seeded and minced
1 bottled pimiento, minced

In top of a double boiler, over simmering water, combine eggs, sugar and vinegar. Cook and stir until thick. Transfer mixture to a medium bowl. Add butter and cream cheese, and beat, with electric mixer, until thoroughly combined. Add hot pepper sauce, onion, green pepper and pimiento. Cover and refrigerate overnight. Serve chilled.

Homemade Boursin with Scallions and Parsley

~

MAKES 2 1/2 CUPS / PREPARATION TIME: 15 MINUTES
CHILLING TIME: OVERNIGHT

Food writer Mara Reid Rogers spent two years devising creative ways to use the most pungent relatives of the lily for her cookbook, *Onions*. A favorite is this takeoff on Boursin cheese: a soft, herbed cheese spread. For an outdoor party, she offers this serving tip: Pack it in a new, brightly colored plastic flower pot lined with wax paper, stick a plant marker labeled with the recipe name in the spread, and fill the plant saucer with crackers.

12 ounces light cream cheese
3/4 cup lowfat small curd cottage cheese
2 teaspoons crushed garlic (put through a garlic press)
1/2 cup thinly sliced scallions
1/3 cup minced parsley (preferably Italian flat-leaf)
salt and freshly cracked black pepper to taste

In a medium bowl, with a wooden spoon or an electric mixer, blend the cream cheese with the cottage cheese. Stir in the garlic, scallions and parsley. Season with salt and black pepper. Transfer to a serving container. Cover and refrigerate, preferably overnight, until ready to serve.

Creamy Mint Dip

~

MAKES 2 CUPS / PREPARATION TIME: 5 MINUTES
CHILLING TIME: 1 HOUR

How could anything so simple taste so good? This cool, creamy dip is just the thing for a spring bridal shower or graduation party, served with blanched baby carrots, sugar snaps, raw turnip slices or jicama sticks. Or, serve it with fresh fruit, such as strawberries, orange sections or pineapple chunks.

2 cups sour cream
3 to 4 tablespoons sugar

2 tablespoons fresh chopped mint (or to taste)
mint sprigs for garnish (optional)

In a medium bowl, whisk together the sour cream and sugar. Fold in mint. Adjust sugar or mint, if desired. Cover and refrigerate until ready to serve. Garnish with mint sprigs.

Blender Salad Dip

~

MAKES ABOUT 1 2/3 CUPS / PREPARATION TIME: 30 MINUTES / CHILLING TIME: 1 HOUR

Here's what to do with that leftover salad: Whirl it into a tangy, surprisingly creamy dip for any raw vegetable, bread stick or cracker — such as the one that follows.

3 cups coarsely chopped lettuce (iceberg, Romaine, leaf, etc.)
1/4 cup oil-and-vinegar dressing

2 to 4 tablespoons chopped scallions
salt to taste
1/8 teaspoon crumbled dried thyme
1/8 teaspoon crumbled dried sage
4 to 8 ounces cheddar cheese, diced

In a blender or food processor, combine 1 cup of lettuce with dressing, scallion, salt, thyme and sage. Whirl until smooth. With machine running, gradually add remaining lettuce and the cheese, blending until smooth. Transfer to a serving bowl. Cover and refrigerate until ready to serve.

Salad Crackers

MAKES ABOUT 24 CRACKERS / PREPARATION TIME: 35 MINUTES

1 1/2 cups all-purpose flour
2 teaspoons sesame seeds
1 1-ounce package (1/4 cup) dry ranch salad dressing mix
1/2 cup rolled oats
1/2 cup water
1/4 cup canola or vegetable oil
Vegetable oil spray

Preheat oven to 350 degrees. Combine all ingredients except vegetable oil spray. Stir to form a soft dough. Knead 5 or 6 times to evenly distribute ingredients. Lightly sprinkle work surface with flour. Pat dough into rectangle. Use rolling pin to even the dough to 1/8-inch thickness. Cut dough lengthwise in 1-inch widths, then crosswise into 2-inch lengths. Spray baking sheet with vegetable oil spray. Arrange cracker dough pieces with 1/2-inch space between them. Bake until just beginning to brown, about 10 to 15 minutes. Store in an airtight container for up to 3 days.

Fireside Dips

~

Americans are fickle when it comes to fondue. Every few years, the trend-trackers report that the 1960s social cliché is back in fashion, but it's just a matter of time before those sleek, new-and-improved fork-and-cauldron sets start populating yard sales. Not that we ever lose our taste for hot, gooey dips — especially in the dead of winter. The most enduring of these, however, are considerably less romantic than the bubbling pots of molten cheese and fork-speared crusty bread cubes shared in Alpine chalets. When it comes right down to it, most of us would probably just as soon eat melted Velveeta with canned tomatoes and chilies straight from the Dutch oven or crock pot, with our favorite chips and beer. For more formal occasions, we might polish the chafing dish to serve a luxuriously rich seafood dip enriched with lots of butter or cream cheese.

I've included classic fondue, some variations on those Americanized favorites and a host of others that are perfect for digging into while watching a football game on TV, celebrating the holidays or just warming your bones. (For chocolate fondue and other warm sweets, see "Dessert Dips.")

Swiss Cheese Fondue

~

MAKES ABOUT 2 1/2 CUPS / PREPARATION TIME: 20 MINUTES

L egend has it that a thrifty Swiss shepherd, looking for a way to make a dried-out hunk of cheese and some stale bread edible, had the notion to melt the cheese in a pot with some of his evening's wine and then dip the bread into it. His creation, which came to be known as fondue (from the French word *fondre*, "to melt"), remains a favorite in Switzerland and a frequent fad in the United States. Here is the basic recipe. Besides crusty bread, dippers might be hard rolls, bagels, boiled new potatoes, broccoli, cauliflower, radishes, carrots, cherry tomatoes, mushrooms, apple and pear slices, pineapple chunks or green seedless grapes.

1 pound (4 cups) natural Swiss cheese, coarsely grated
(4 ounces, or 1 cup, shredded Gruyere may be substituted
for part of the Swiss)
3 tablespoons all-purpose flour.
1 clove garlic, peeled and halved
1 cup Sauterne or other dry white wine, plus warm wine to
thin, if necessary
1 tablespoon lemon juice
white pepper, to taste
grated nutmeg, to taste
2 tablespoons kirsch (or cherry brandy)
1 long loaf French bread, cut in thick slices and quartered

Toss cheese with flour and set aside. Rub the inside of a fondue pot or chafing dish with cut sides of garlic clove; discard garlic. Set pot over medium heat on stove top and heat 1 cup wine and lemon juice until hot, but not boiling. When hot, begin adding cheese by the handful, stirring constantly in one direction with a wooden spoon. Maintain medium heat, but do not boil. Let each handful melt and become thoroughly incorporated before adding more. Make sure heat is distributed evenly; otherwise cheese can coagulate in the center. If this happens, it is better to start over rather than risk ruining all the cheese. When all the cheese has melted and the mixture is smooth and creamy, season with white pepper and nutmeg. Add kirsch. Transfer pot to fondue burner. Keep warm over low heat as everyone dunks bread in and coats each piece with the bubbling cheese mixture. If it gets too thick, add more wine and stir until smooth.

Good Luck Dip

~

MAKES ABOUT 8 CUPS / PREPARATION TIME: 30 MINUTES

I don't put a lot of stock in that old Southern superstition that eating black-eyed peas on New Year's Day will ensure a prosperous new year, but it never hurts to include them on the menu just in case. And they don't go down any easier than in this rich, cheesy dip laced with jalapeño peppers. Serve with tortilla chips or corn chips.

3 16-ounce cans black-eyed peas, drained
  (or about 4 cups cooked and drained)
5 jalapeño peppers, seeded and chopped
1/2 cup chopped onion
1 clove garlic, peeled and minced
1 cup (2 sticks) butter, melted
1 4-ounce can chopped green chilies, undrained
2 cups (8 ounces) shredded Monterey Jack cheese
1 cup chopped tomatoes
jalapeno pepper slices, tomato wedges for garnish (optional)

Preheat oven to 325 degrees. In a blender or food processor, combine peas, peppers, onion and garlic, and puree. Fold in butter. Pour mixture into a 3-quart baking dish. Top with chilies and their juice, and cheese. Heat in oven until cheese melts, about 10 to 15 minutes. Garnish with jalapeno pepper slices and tomato wedges. Serve hot.

Hot Broccoli-Almond Dip

~

MAKES ABOUT 4 CUPS / PREPARATION TIME: 25 MINUTES

There is nothing nouvelle about this dip — it's a lot like the church-supper casseroles of decades past that were loaded with enough butter, canned soup and processed cheese to negate any possible health benefits of whatever vegetables they contained. But, boy, does it taste good! Make it a day ahead if you like, cover and refrigerate. Heat through in the microwave. Sturdy crackers and vegetables make fine dippers. Toss leftovers with macaroni or small shell pasta.

1/2 cup slivered almonds
1/2 cup (1 stick) butter
1 small onion, chopped
1 10-ounce package frozen broccoli, thawed and chopped
1 7-ounce can sliced mushrooms, drained
1 10 3/4-ounce can cream of mushroom soup (undiluted)
6 ounces nippy cheese, or processed cheese spread, cut into chunks
1/4 teaspoon garlic powder
1/4 teaspoon black pepper
3 shakes hot pepper sauce
small, cooked broccoli spears for garnish (optional)

In a heavy, ungreased skillet, over medium heat, toast almonds until golden brown, about 3 minutes, stirring constantly. In a medium saucepan, over medium heat, melt butter. Stir in onion and sauté until golden, about 2 minutes. Stir in remaining ingredients. Cook for 5 to 10 minutes, until cheese is thoroughly melted and mixture is hot and bubbling. Transfer to a serving bowl. Garnish with broccoli spears. Serve hot.

Beer-Cheese Fondue

~

MAKES ABOUT 3 1/3 CUPS / PREPARATION TIME: 30 MINUTES

These hearty flavors are a perfect match for rye or pumpernickel bread, both of which can be used as edible bowls for the dip. Use the bread's interior, cut in chunks, as dippers. Or, chill the fondue and serve as a spread. Rye crackers, pretzels and raw carrots are also good for dipping.

> *2 tablespoons butter or margarine, softened*
> *1/2 small onion, finely chopped*
> *1 tablespoon Worcestershire sauce*
> *1 teaspoon hot pepper sauce*
> *1/4 teaspoon garlic powder*
> *1 1/2 pounds sharp cheddar cheese spread*
>   *(for extra bite, use jalapeño-flavored)*
> *3/4 cup (3 ounces) crumbled blue cheese*
> *1/2 to 1 cup beer*
> *1 unsliced loaf round rye bread for serving (optional)*

In a medium saucepan, over medium heat, melt butter. Add onion and sauté until soft. Add Worcestershire, hot pepper sauce and garlic powder, reduce heat to medium-low, and add cheddar cheese spread a little at a time to melt. Gradually add blue cheese and enough beer for desired consistency. Continue to cook and stir until mixture is entirely melted. If using bread bowl, prepare it by first slicing off the top, then scooping out the insides, leaving a thick crust intact. Cut the scooped-out bread into cubes for dipping. Pour cheese mixture in shell and serve hot as a dip. Or, replace the top and refrigerate. Bring to room temperature 30 minutes before serving and use as a spread.

Hot-cha-cha Black Bean Dip

~

MAKES 2 CUPS / PREPARATION TIME: 20 MINUTES

Black beans lend a Cuban twist to this spicy, cheesy dip for tortilla and other chips.

1 15-ounce can black beans,
  rinsed and drained
1 tablespoon lemon or lime juice
1 to 2 large cloves garlic,
  pressed (with a garlic press)

1/2 cup sour cream
1 to 2 tablespoons chopped green chilies
1 1/2 cups (6 ounces) grated Monterey
  Jack cheese with jalapeño peppers
cilantro sprigs for garnish (optional)

In a food processor or blender, combine all ingredients except cheese and garnish. Blend until smooth. Transfer to a 1-quart microwave-safe bowl. Add cheese and stir. Cover and microwave on HIGH for 2 to 4 minutes, or until cheese is melted. Garnish with cilantro sprigs. Serve hot.

Killer Queso

~

MAKES 3 1/2 CUPS / PREPARATION TIME: 20 MINUTES

In Texas, says *Austin American-Statesman* food editor Kitty Crider, it's hard to have a party or watch a ball game without queso. Here is one of the most popular versions. Serve with corn chips or tortilla chips. Leftovers are terrific on a baked potato or broccoli.

1 pound hot bulk pork sausage
1 pound Velveeta cheese, cubed

1 10-ounce can tomatoes with chilies (such as Ro-Tel brand),
or 1 8-ounce jar of picante sauce

In a Dutch oven, brown sausage. Drain grease. Add cheese and tomatoes. Heat, stirring, over low heat until cheese is melted.

Or, after browning sausage, heat ingredients in a crock pot. Or, combine them in a microwavable dish and microwave on HIGH for 6 to 8 minutes, stirring every few minutes.

Baked Fiesta Spinach Dip

~

MAKES ABOUT 6 1/2 CUPS / PREPARATION TIME: 45 MINUTES

Probably the only person in Georgia who's racked up more prizes for cooking than Bessie Burk is her daughter, Mary Louise Lever (see Caribbean Eggnog Dip, page 133). This creation of Bessie's is colorful, easy, different and almost impossible to stop eating. Serve with any kind of chip.

1 cup chopped onion
1 tablespoon vegetable oil
1 cup chunky salsa, well-drained
1 10-ounce package chopped spinach, thawed and squeezed dry

2 1/2 cups (10 ounces) shredded Monterey Jack cheese
8 ounces light cream cheese, cubed
1 cup light cream
1/2 cup sliced black olives
1 cup chopped pecans

Preheat oven to 400 degrees. In a medium skillet, over medium heat, sauté onion in oil until tender. Stir in salsa and spinach, cooking 2 minutes more. Transfer to a 1 1/2-quart baking dish. Stir in 2 cups Monterey Jack cheese, the cream cheese, cream and olives. Sprinkle with pecans. Bake about 30 minutes or until hot and bubbly (cover with foil during last 15 minutes to prevent burning). Top with remaining Monterey Jack cheese. Serve hot.

Hot Creole Seafood Dip

~

MAKES ABOUT 3 CUPS / PREPARATION TIME: 45 MINUTES

Caterer Les Carloss is best known for the specialties he's put on menus in five New Orleans-style restaurants he's opened in San Diego and Atlanta. Even the dips he serves have a Creole twist, like this one which features crawfish, spicy seasonings and the Holy Trinity of Creole cooking: onions, celery and green bell pepper. This is a somewhat less rich adaptation of the recipe as it appears in his cookbook, *The Best of Creole Cooking*. If you can't get crawfish, shrimp works just as well. Serve with crackers or toast points.

2 ounces (1/2 stick) butter
1/2 cup finely chopped yellow onion
1/2 cup finely chopped scallions
1/2 cup finely chopped celery
1/2 cup finely chopped green bell pepper
1 teaspoon finely minced garlic
8 ounces cream cheese
8 ounces crawfish tail meat or diced, cooked shrimp
1/2 pound fresh crabmeat (or 2 6-ounce cans, drained)
2 tablespoons mayonnaise
1 teaspoon Creole or Old Bay seasoning
1 teaspoon dry mustard
1 teaspoon hot pepper sauce
3 tablespoons dry sherry
salt to taste

In a large skillet, over medium-high heat, melt the butter. Add yellow onion, scallions, celery, bell pepper and garlic. Sauté for about 5 minutes, or until vegetables are soft and most of liquid has evaporated. Reduce heat to medium-low and add cheese, crawfish and crabmeat. Cook until cheese is melted. Add remaining ingredients. Simmer and stir until well blended. Transfer to a 1 1/2-quart serving dish. Serve hot.

New Jersey Hot Crab Dip

MAKES ABOUT 4 CUPS / PREPARATION TIME: 45 MINUTES

Here's a hot seafood dip with a Jersey accent.

> *1 pound fresh, thawed frozen or canned crabmeat, drained*
> *1 tablespoon prepared horseradish*
> *1/2 of a 3-ounce bottle capers, drained*
> *1 tablespoon grated lemon zest (colored part of lemon)*
> *1/2 teaspoon Accent (optional)*
> *dash of hot pepper sauce*
> *1 tablespoon Worcestershire sauce*
> *2 cups mayonnaise*
> *1/4 teaspoon garlic powder (or to taste)*
> *3/4 cup (3 ounces) grated cheddar cheese*

Preheat oven to 300 degrees. In a large bowl, combine all ingredients except cheese. Pour mixture into shallow 2-quart casserole dish. Top with cheese. Bake for 20 to 25 minutes, until heated through. Serve hot.

Reuben Dip

~

MAKES ABOUT 1 1/2 CUPS / PREPARATION TIME: 25 MINUTES

New York deli meets Swiss fondue in this hearty concoction that was made for rye and pumpernickel crackers or bread cubes.

> *3 ounces cream cheese*
> *1/4 cup sour cream*
> *4 ounces sliced corned beef, finely chopped*
> *1/2 cup (2 ounces) grated Swiss cheese*
> *1/4 cup drained and chopped sauerkraut*
> *2 or 3 tablespoons milk (optional)*

In a small saucepan, combine cream cheese, sour cream, corned beef, Swiss cheese and sauerkraut. Simmer over low heat for 10 to 15 minutes, or until hot. Thin with milk, if desired. Transfer to a serving dish. Serve hot.

Pepperoni Pizza Dip

~

MAKES 1 9-INCH PIE / PREPARATION TIME: 30 MINUTES

Too bad Domino's doesn't deliver this one. The good news, though, is that it's no big deal to make, even on a couch-potato kind of night. And chances are you've already got the ingredients. Vary the toppings according to whatever you're craving. Dig in with Italian bread sticks, melba toast or ridged potato chips. Or spread it on chunks of Boboli prepared pizza crust.

8 ounces cream cheese, softened
1 14-ounce jar pizza sauce
1/3 cup chopped onions
1 1/2 cups (6 ounces) grated mozzarella cheese
1 6-ounce can black olives, chopped
2 ounces sliced pepperoni, chopped

Preheat oven to 350 degrees. Spread cream cheese in bottom of a 9-inch ungreased glass pie plate. Spread pizza sauce over cream cheese and layer onions, mozzarella cheese, olives and pepperoni in order. Bake for 20 to 25 minutes. Serve hot.

Sombrero Spread

MAKES 2 1/2 CUPS / PREPARATION TIME: 30 MINUTES

Chili on a chip: That's pretty much what this boils down to. It's practically a meal in itself.

1/2 pound ground beef
1 cup chopped onion
1/4 cup hot ketchup (or 1/4 cup regular ketchup and hot pepper sauce to taste)
1 1/2 teaspoons chili powder
1/2 teaspoon salt
1 16-ounce can kidney beans, undrained
1/2 cup (2 ounces) shredded sharp cheddar cheese
1/4 cup chopped pimiento-stuffed green olives

In a medium skillet, over medium heat, or in a chafing dish, brown meat and 3/4 cup onion. Drain off excess grease. Stir in ketchup, chili powder and salt. Mash in beans and liquid, and heat through. Top with cheese, olives and remaining onion. Serve hot from skillet or chafing dish.

Warm Mushroom and Bacon Dip

~

MAKES 2 1/2 CUPS / PREPARATION TIME: 20 MINUTES

Here's a glorified version of the dried onion soup classic, served warm. Toss leftovers with warm pasta or spoon on a baked potato. The only better dipper for it than plain old potato chips may be the homemade Spicy Potato Skins that follow.

6 slices bacon
8 ounces thinly sliced mushrooms
2 cloves garlic, finely chopped
1 envelope dry onion soup mix (1.15 ounces)
1 cup light cream cheese
1 cup light sour cream

In a skillet, over medium-high heat, cook bacon. Remove bacon from pan and crumble. Drain grease, leaving about 1 tablespoon in the skillet. Add mushrooms and garlic. Cook over medium heat, stirring occasionally, for 5 minutes. Add onion soup mix and cream cheese. Stir in sour cream and bacon, and heat through. Transfer to a serving bowl. Serve warm.

Spicy Potato Skins: Preheat oven to 400 degrees. Prick 4 large baking potatoes with a fork. Bake potatoes for 45 minutes to 1 hour, or until soft. Remove from oven. Lower oven temperature to 375 degrees. Let potatoes cool to room temperature. Cut potatoes in half crosswise. Cut each half into lengthwise quarters. Remove the inside of the potato, leaving about 1/4 inch on the skin. Brush soy sauce on both sides. Spray vegetable oil on both sides. Arrange on a baking sheet, skin side down, and sprinkle with chili powder to taste. Bake for 20 minutes or until crisp and brown. Serve immediately or cover tightly and refrigerate. Heat when ready to serve. Makes 32.

Texas Crabgrass

~

MAKES 2 1/2 CUPS / PREPARATION TIME: 20 MINUTES

Texans know the best way to get rid of this kind of crabgrass — with lots of crackers for dipping. Try pastel-colored shrimp chips or crab-flavored crackers, found in Asian markets, for something different.

1/4 cup (1/2 stick) butter or margarine
1/2 cup chopped onion
1 10-ounce package frozen chopped spinach,
  cooked and drained
1 6- to 7-ounce can crabmeat, flaked
3/4 cup grated Parmesan cheese
1 cup sour cream

In a heavy saucepan, over medium heat, melt butter. Add onion and sauté until soft and golden. Stir in remaining ingredients and cook just long enough to heat through. Transfer to serving dish. Serve warm.

Holiday Ham Dip

~

MAKES ABOUT 3 CUPS / PREPARATION TIME: 30 MINUTES

Brighten up your holiday buffet table with this colorful, pecan-studded dip that goes particularly well with rye or wheat crackers, as well as broccoli, cauliflower, bell peppers and Brussels sprouts.

8 ounces cream cheese, softened
8 ounces sour cream
1/3 pound deli-style Virginia baked ham, finely chopped
1/4 cup diced green bell pepper
1/4 cup finely chopped red onion
2 tablespoons chopped pimiento
1/2 teaspoon garlic powder
1/4 teaspoon ground white pepper
1/8 teaspoon freshly grated nutmeg
1/2 cup chopped pecans

Preheat oven to 350 degrees. In a medium bowl, blend cream cheese and sour cream. Stir in ham, bell pepper, onion, pimiento, garlic powder, white pepper and nutmeg. Pour mixture into a 1-quart rectangular baking dish. Top with pecans. Bake for 20 to 25 minutes, or until heated through. Serve hot.

Hot Honey Hummus Dip

~

MAKES ABOUT 5 CUPS / PREPARATION TIME: 45 MINUTES

The Middle Eastern chickpea spread, hummus, isn't typically served hot — but then, this isn't your typical hummus. Tofu gives it a creamier consistency; a drizzle of honey offsets the tang of the feta cheese, the fire of the spices and the tartness of the limes. Serve with pita chips or bagel chips.

1 19-ounce can (2 cups) chickpeas, drained
2 cups (8 ounces) crumbled feta cheese
8 ounces soft or firm tofu, drained
1/4 cup olive oil
1 medium onion, chopped
3 tablespoons soft bread crumbs
3 tablespoons chopped parsley
1 tablespoon ground cumin
1 teaspoon ground red pepper
1 teaspoon salt
juice of 2 limes
nonstick vegetable spray
1/4 cup honey
lime slices for garnish (optional)

Preheat oven to 350 degrees. In a blender or food processor, puree chickpeas, feta cheese, tofu and olive oil. Add onion, bread crumbs, parsley, cumin, red pepper, salt and lime juice. Puree until smooth. Coat a 13-by-9-by-2-inch casserole dish with nonstick vegetable spray. Spread mixture in dish. Bake, uncovered, for 20 to 30 minutes, or until heated through. Remove from oven. Pour thin line of honey on surface in lattice design. Garnish with lime slices. Serve hot or at room temperature.

Blue Hawaii Dip

~

MAKES ABOUT 2 CUPS / PREPARATION TIME: 30 MINUTES

Cook an extra fish fillet for dinner tonight and give this deliciously different dip from Hawaii a shot for tomorrow's party. Offer sea-salt bagel chips and buttery crackers.

2 tablespoons butter or margarine
1/2 cup chopped macadamia nuts
6- to 8-ounce mahi mahi fillet (or other flaky white fish
*   fillet such as catfish or orange roughy)*
1 teaspoon lemon juice
1/4 cup blue cheese dressing
3 ounces cream cheese
1/2 cup sour cream
2 tablespoons milk

Preheat oven to 350 degrees. In a skillet, over medium heat, melt the butter. Add nuts and, stirring occasionally, sauté until golden. Set aside. Bake fish for about 7 minutes, or until cooked through. Cool and shred into flakes. In a medium bowl, mix fish with remaining ingredients except nuts. Transfer mixture to a shallow baking dish. Spread nuts on mixture. Bake at 350 degrees for about 10 to 15 minutes, until heated through. Serve hot.

Baked Artichoke Dip

~

MAKES 2 CUPS / PREPARATION TIME: 30 MINUTES

You've probably already got a version of this recipe in your recipe box — everyone else does — but a dip book just wouldn't be complete without it. In its most basic form, it consists of artichoke hearts, mayonnaise and Parmesan cheese, mixed together in a pan and baked. I like this one better; it has some cream cheese substituting for part of the mayonnaise, a hefty dose of garlic and a crunchy bread-crumb topping. Besides melba toast and chips, consider fresh-cooked artichoke leaves for dipping.

> *3 large cloves garlic, peeled*
> *1 14-ounce can artichoke hearts, drained*
> *1/2 cup plus 2 tablespoons (about 2 1/2 ounces)*
> * finely grated Parmesan cheese*
> *2 tablespoons white wine*
> *1 tablespoon lemon juice*
> *1/4 cup mayonnaise*
> *1/4 cup cream cheese, softened*
> *3 tablespoons dry bread crumbs*

Preheat oven to 375 degrees. In a food processor, with the machine running, drop garlic cloves through the chute and process until minced. Add artichoke hearts. Pulse several times until finely chopped. In a medium bowl, combine the 1/2 cup Parmesan cheese, the wine, lemon juice, mayonnaise and cream cheese. Stir in the garlic-artichoke mixture. Transfer to a 1-quart casserole dish. Sprinkle with bread crumbs and remaining Parmesan cheese. Bake until bubbly, about 20 minutes. Serve hot.

Black Tie Dips

~

There are dips that are most at home in Tupperware containers . . . and then there are dips that are fit for a silver tray. It's all in the ingredients: Substitute caviar for the dried soup mix, and that sour cream concoction is ready for the ball. Roquefort, goat cheese, smoked salmon, lobster, Marsala, port — these are just a few of the tastes that find their way into the elegant dips and spreads that follow.

Presentation is important here, too. Some are molded into fancy shapes, packed into classy crocks or crystal bowls, or garnished into edible works of art. Not that they're difficult to make — most, in fact, are so simple, the quality ingredients speak for themselves.

If you're getting ready to throw a gala, don't ignore the offerings elsewhere — the Tapenade in the "Worldly Dips" chapter and the Tiramisu Dip in "Dessert Dips" are just a couple of others that are also dressed for the occasion.

Sage and Walnut
Goat Cheese Spread

~

MAKES 1 1/2 CUPS / PREPARATION TIME: 10 MINUTES
STANDING TIME: 30 MINUTES

Smooth, slightly tart goat cheese provides the basis for some of the most luxurious dips and spreads. Like the more pedestrian cream cheese, its character can change with the seasons, depending on how you dress it. For fall, an embellishment of walnuts and sage makes it a perfect partner for apples, pears and other autumn flavors. (For summer, try the Goat Cheese Dip With Bell Pepper and Chives on page 4.)

1 tablespoon unsalted butter
1 cup chopped walnuts
1/4 teaspoon salt
1 teaspoon crushed, dried sage
4 ounces goat cheese
2 tablespoons heavy cream
sage leaves, walnut halves for garnish (optional)

In a skillet, over medium-low heat, melt butter. Add walnuts and salt. Sauté until golden. Transfer to a bowl. By hand, blend the walnuts and sage into the goat cheese, adding cream for a smoother texture. Cover and refrigerate. Let stand for 30 minutes at room temperature before serving. Garnish with sage leaves and walnut halves.

Tarragon-Chicken Pâté

～

MAKES 2 1/2 CUPS / PREPARATION TIME: 25 MINUTES
CHILLING TIME: 2 HOURS

One of my favorite pâtés contains no liver and is made instead with chicken breast meat. Port or sherry and tarragon impart an elegant flavor, a little cream cheese a silky consistency. Store in the refrigerator for up to five days or in freezer for two to three months. Spread on crackers, melba toast or thinly sliced French bread.

1/4 cup (1/2 stick) butter
1 cup sliced onion
6 uncooked boneless, skinless chicken breast halves,
   cut in chunks
1 cup tawny port wine or dry sherry, divided
3 ounces cream cheese, softened
2 tablespoons milk or cream
1 1/4 teaspoons crumbled leaf tarragon
salt and black pepper to taste
1 cup slivered almonds, toasted
paprika for garnish (optional)

In a skillet, over medium heat, melt butter. Add onion and sauté until tender. Add chicken pieces and continue to sauté, stirring frequently, until chicken loses its pink color on outside. Add 1/2 cup of port or sherry. Bring to a boil. Reduce to medium heat and cook at a rolling boil, uncovered, just until chicken is done and liquid is reduced by about half. Transfer mixture to a blender or food processor and puree. Add cream cheese, milk, tarragon, salt, pepper and remaining 1/2 cup port or sherry. Process until smooth. Add almonds, reserving some for garnish, and process until smooth. Pack firmly into a decorative crock. Cover and refrigerate for up to 5 days. Garnish with reserved almonds and paprika.

Caviar Pie

MAKES 1 9-INCH PIE / PREPARATION TIME: 20 MINUTES

Here is a dip so stunning to look at, even caviar haters have been persuaded to dig in. Atop a simple cream cheese and sour cream base, a bull's-eye of black caviar is surrounded by concentric circles of chopped egg, scallion, red salmon caviar and parsley — a taste combination as appealing as the design. Surround with crackers, melba toast or pumpernickel rounds.

> 8 ounces cream cheese, softened
> 1/4 cup sour cream
> 1 2-ounce jar black caviar
> 4 hard-boiled egg yolks, chopped or sieved
> 5 scallion tops, finely chopped
> 1 3 1/2-ounce jar red salmon caviar
> 4 hard-boiled egg whites, chopped or sieved
> 1/3 cup finely chopped parsley

In a medium bowl, whip cream cheese with sour cream until fluffy. In a 9-inch glass pie plate, spread the mixture. In the center of the cream cheese mixture, mound black caviar. Surround with circle of egg yolks, then scallions, red salmon caviar, egg whites and parsley. Cover loosely and refrigerate until ready to use.

Marsala-Lobster Spread

~

MAKES 3 CUPS / PREPARATION TIME: 20 MINUTES
CHILLING TIME: SEVERAL HOURS

A signature hors d'oeuvre from Chef's Expressions Catering in Timonium, Maryland, is this eye-catching spread. Chef Jerry Edwards typically molds it into a lobster shape and decorates with scallion antennae and lemon slices for shells, then sprinkles with paprika. Other shellfish can fill in for the lobster. Serve with crackers or toasted baguette slices.

1 pound (2 8-ounce packages) cream cheese
4 ounces (1 stick) unsalted butter, slightly softened
2 tablespoons minced onion
2 tablespoons Marsala wine
pinch of turmeric
1/2 pound lobster meat, cooked, drained
  and coarsely chopped
scallions, lemon slices, paprika for garnish (optional)

In a large bowl, with a wooden spoon, blend the cream cheese, butter, onion, wine and turmeric. Fold in the lobster. Line a lobster mold, or other seaside motif, with plastic wrap and fill with mixture. Cover with plastic wrap and refrigerate for several hours. Remove from mold when ready to serve.

Chicken Liver and Golden Raisin Pâté

~

MAKES ABOUT 2 CUPS / PREPARATION TIME: 50 MINUTES
CHILLING TIME: 2 HOURS

This voluptuous pâté has a hint of sweetness, which makes it a perfect match for autumn pears and apples, besides the usual toast points.

1/4 cup (1/2 stick) unsalted butter
1 large onion, sliced
salt and pepper to taste
1 tablespoon dried thyme
1 pound chicken livers, trimmed of connective tissue,
*   rinsed and drained*
1 cup dry sherry
1/4 cup golden raisins
1 tablespoon brown sugar
1/4 cup heavy cream

In a heavy skillet, over medium heat, melt butter. Add onion. Stir until coated. Reduce heat to low and cook onion, stirring frequently, until soft and caramelized, about 30 minutes. With a slotted spoon, transfer onion to a food processor. Increase heat under skillet to medium. Add chicken livers, salt, pepper and thyme. Sauté livers until they lose their pink color, about 5 minutes. Transfer chicken livers to the food processor. Increase heat under skillet to high. Add sherry. Scraping the bottom of the skillet, cook until sherry is reduced by half, about 5 minutes. Add raisins, brown sugar and cream to skillet and turn heat to low. Cook for 3 minutes. Transfer mixture to the food processor. Puree, with onion and chicken livers, until well blended. Transfer to a serving bowl. Cover and refrigerate for 2 hours before serving.

Blue Cheese, Grape and Walnut Spread

~

MAKES 3 CUPS / PREPARATION TIME: 10 MINUTES
CHILLING TIME: 30 MINUTES TO OVERNIGHT

My colleague Kristin Eddy got the idea for this dip after dining on a salad of the same ingredients at Luna Si, an Atlanta restaurant. There, julienned jicama was topped with crumbled blue cheese and walnuts, and surrounded by red grapes. Here, jicama is recommended for scooping. Or, dip with apple slices or wheat crackers.

1 cup walnut halves
2 cups (8 ounces) crumbled blue cheese
2 tablespoons port or dry sherry
2 tablespoons heavy cream
1 cup seedless red grapes, rinsed and patted dry
walnut halves, grapes for garnish (optional)

In an ungreased heavy skillet, over medium heat, toast walnuts, stirring constantly, until golden, about 3 minutes. They should have lost their raw taste. Immediately transfer to a bowl to cool. After about 5 minutes, coarsely chop walnuts. Set aside. In a food processor, blend cheese, port and cream to a smooth paste. Add grapes. Pulse until grapes are chopped and distributed throughout mixture. Scrape mixture into a serving bowl. Stir in chopped nuts. Cover tightly and refrigerate for 30 minutes to overnight. Serve cool or at room temperature.

Brandied Blue Cheese Spread

~

MAKES 1 1/2 CUPS / PREPARATION TIME: 10 MINUTES
CHILLING TIME: SEVERAL HOURS (PREFERABLY OVERNIGHT)

Brandy and pecans take this dip in a different direction. Serve on a celery stick or radicchio leaf.

1/4 cup (1/2 stick) unsalted butter, softened
4 ounces cream cheese, at room temperature
1 cup (4 ounces) crumbled blue cheese
4 teaspoons mayonnaise
2 tablespoons brandy or cognac
dash of Worcestershire sauce
1/2 cup finely chopped pecans

In a medium bowl, mix butter, cream cheese and blue cheese. Add mayonnaise, brandy and Worcestershire sauce. Beat until blended. Stir in pecans. Cover and refrigerate for several hours, preferably overnight, to blend flavors. Remove from the refrigerator 30 minutes before serving.

Pistachio-Cheese Log

~

MAKES 1 8-INCH LOG / PREPARATION TIME: 30 MINUTES
CHILLING TIME: 3 HOURS

Cheese logs and cheese balls have been common cocktail party fare for at least a half-century; even further back, bite-size cheese balls were often served as an accompaniment to ladies' luncheon salads. Most start with cream cheese, with some shredded sharp cheddar cheese, and perhaps a flavoring of some sort — a splash of port, some minced vegetable, a little dry mustard. One of the easiest I've heard of is to blend together an 8-ounce package of cream cheese with a packet of dry ranch salad dressing mix, form it in a ball and roll the whole thing in chopped pecans. This one, a creation of the Philadelphia Brand Cream Cheese folks, is a little more work than that, but is still pretty easy in the big scheme of things. It's a fine addition to a cheese board, to show folks that you went to at least a little effort. Serve with a buttery cracker.

1 1/2 cups (6 ounces) shredded sharp cheddar cheese
8 ounces cream cheese, softened
2 tablespoons finely chopped scallion
2 tablespoons finely chopped red bell pepper
1 clove garlic, finely minced
2 teaspoons white wine Worcestershire sauce
1/2 cup (2 ounces) crumbled blue cheese
2 tablespoons milk
1/3 cup finely chopped red or natural pistachio nuts

In a medium bowl, with an electric mixer, beat cheddar cheese and 4 ounces cream cheese at medium speed until blended. Mix in scallion, bell pepper, garlic and Worcestershire sauce. Refrigerate for 30 minutes. In another medium bowl, with an electric mixer, beat remaining 4 ounces cream cheese, the blue cheese and milk at medium speed until blended. Shape chilled cheddar cheese mixture into an 8-inch log. Spread blue cheese mixture evenly on top and sides of log. Cover with pistachio nuts. Wrap in plastic wrap and refrigerate for several hours. Serve cold or at room temperature.

Pesto, Salmon and Cream Cheese Loaf

~

MAKES A 9-BY-5-BY-3-INCH LOAF / PREPARATION TIME: 30 MINUTES
CHILLING TIME: AT LEAST 6 HOURS

Layered cheese loaves make easy, dramatic presentations. Simply blend a mixture of butter and cream cheese, then layer it with colorful, intensely flavored goodies. Try pesto and smoked salmon. Chopped sun-dried tomatoes in oil would also pair beautifully with the pesto. Or use olivada — an olive paste found in gourmet markets — instead of the pesto.

2 pounds (4 8-ounce packages) cream cheese,
   at room temperature, divided
1 cup (2 sticks) unsalted butter, at room temperature
7 ounces pesto
6 ounces smoked salmon, finely chopped
black olive slices, fresh basil leaves as garnish (optional)

In a medium bowl, with an electric mixer, blend 24 ounces (3 packages) cream cheese with the butter. In a second bowl, mix 4 ounces (1/2 package) cream cheese and the pesto. In a third bowl, mix 4 ounces (1/2 package) cream cheese and the salmon. Line a 9-by-5-by-3-inch loaf pan with plastic wrap, large enough to cover the loaf later. Spread a third of cream cheese-butter mixture in pan. Top with cream cheese-pesto mixture. Top with another third of the cream cheese-butter mixture. Top with cream cheese-salmon mixture. Top with remaining cream cheese-butter mixture. Fold plastic wrap over to enclose, press firmly and refrigerate for at least 6 hours. When ready to serve, fold back plastic wrap and turn out onto platter. Garnish with olives and basil leaves.

Ricotta-Pesto Mousse

~

MAKES ABOUT 3 CUPS / PREPARATION TIME: 15 MINUTES
CHILLING TIME: 2 HOURS PLUS OVERNIGHT

Mixing cream cheese with ricotta lightens the texture, and makes a creamy contrast to the homemade pesto sauce (though commercial, of course, could be substituted).

This is considerably softer than the preceding loaf, so dip with your favorite vegetables, or skewered tortellini, along with bread sticks or crackers. (You should have at least 1/2 cup pesto left; refrigerate and toss with pasta later.)

8 ounces light cream cheese
8 ounces light ricotta cheese
2 cups fresh basil leaves
1/4 cup olive oil
2 to 3 cloves garlic
1 tablespoon broken walnuts
2 tablespoons grated Parmesan cheese
1/4 teaspoon salt
olive oil or olive oil spray, for coating
fresh basil leaves for garnish (optional)

On a baking sheet, spread a tea towel or a triple layer of cheesecloth. In a medium bowl, with an electric mixer, beat cream cheese and ricotta until thoroughly combined. Form the mixture into two approximately 6-inch rounds on the toweling, smoothing the tops. Refrigerate uncovered for 2 hours. Meanwhile, make pesto: In a food processor, combine basil, 1/4 cup olive oil, garlic, walnuts, Parmesan cheese and salt. Puree to a paste. On a serving plate, place one cheese round and coat lightly with olive oil. Spread with about 1/2 cup of the pesto, almost to edges. Place second round on top, sealing and smoothing edges. Garnish with fresh basil leaves. Wrap tightly in plastic wrap and refrigerate overnight.

Low Country Shrimp Paste

MAKES 3 1/2 CUPS / PREPARATION TIME: 35 MINUTES
CHILLING TIME: 2 HOURS

If you like shrimp, you'll love this dip. Fresh shrimp is the main ingredient, with just enough mayonnaise to bind it together and a few other simple ingredients to enhance its natural flavor. Serve in a crystal bowl, with buttery crackers or water biscuits.

3 pounds shrimp, cooked,
  peeled and deveined
1/2 to 3/4 cup mayonnaise
2 tablespoons grated onion

2 tablespoons Worcestershire sauce
2 tablespoons lemon juice
1 teaspoon salt
1/8 teaspoon ground red pepper

In a blender or food processor, chop shrimp. Blend in enough mayonnaise to moisten. Stir in onion, Worcestershire sauce, lemon juice, salt and red pepper. Transfer to a serving bowl. Cover and refrigerate for a few hours to blend flavors.

Smoked Trout Dip

MAKES 2 CUPS / PREPARATION TIME: 10 MINUTES
CHILLING TIME: 1 HOUR

Any smoked fish will work in this easy dip. Trout is outstanding. Serve with cucumber slices and crackers.

1/2 cup sour cream
8 ounces cream cheese, softened
4 dashes hot pepper sauce
2 teaspoons Worcestershire sauce

1/2 pound smoked trout fillets,
  skinned and boned
1/2 cup chopped scallions

In a medium bowl, blend sour cream, cream cheese, Worcestershire sauce and hot pepper sauce until smooth. Transfer to a serving bowl. Break fillets into large pieces and stir into dip, allowing some chunks to remain for texture. Gently stir in all but 2 tablespoons of the scallions. Cover and refrigerate for 1 hour. Garnish with remaining scallions.

Smoked Salmon Dip

MAKES ABOUT 4 CUPS / PREPARATION TIME: 10 MINUTES
CHILLING TIME: 30 MINUTES TO OVERNIGHT

Smoked salmon, red onion, cream cheese and capers taste just as great blended into a dip as they do layered on a bagel. Bagel chips, of course, make perfect dippers, as do cucumber slices and cherry tomatoes.

1 cup sour cream
1 pound (2 8-ounce packages) cream cheese
1 tablespoon lemon juice
4 or 5 drops hot pepper sauce

1 medium red onion, peeled and coarsely chopped
1/4 cup capers, drained
1/4 pound smoked salmon
chopped parsley, salmon roe for garnish (optional)

In a food processor, blend sour cream, cream cheese, lemon juice and hot pepper sauce until smooth. Add onion, capers and salmon. Puree until smooth. Transfer to a serving bowl. Cover tightly and refrigerate for 30 minutes to overnight. Serve cold, garnished with chopped parsley around the edge of the bowl, and salmon roe in center.

Warm Brie
with Figs and Almonds

~

MAKES 1 8-OUNCE BRIE WHEEL OR WEDGE / PREPARATION TIME: 20 MINUTES
MARINATING TIME: 1 HOUR

When slightly heated, brie softens to spreadable — even dippable — consistency, and is a luxuriously creamy foil to the sandwiched ingredients: sweet dried figs, salty ham and crunchy almonds. This makes a small wheel or wedge — enough for 4 to 8 people, depending upon what else is served — but you could easily multiply the ingredients for a large brie wheel. Spread this on sliced French bread, water biscuits, melba toast or halved fresh figs.

2 tablespoons finely chopped dried figs
2 tablespoons dry sherry
1 8-ounce brie wheel or wedge, very cold
1 tablespoon sliced almonds, toasted
2 tablespoons finely chopped prosciutto or country ham

In a small bowl, combine figs and sherry. Marinate for at least 1 hour. Drain figs and pat dry. Preheat oven to 300 degrees. Slice brie in half horizontally. Spread figs, almonds and ham evenly on one half of cheese. Top with other half. Transfer to a baking sheet. Bake until just heated through and soft, about 10 to 15 minutes. Serve warm.

Brie and Praline Spread

~

Here is a slight variation on the brie theme; this time it's gussied up with caramelized pecans. Serve it as an appetizer or dessert; pair it with apple or pear slices, toasted bread, unsalted crackers or champagne biscuits.

2 tablespoons unsalted butter
1/2 cup chopped pecans
2 tablespoons packed brown sugar
1 8-ounce brie wheel or wedge, very cold

Preheat oven to 350 degrees. In a medium saucepan, melt butter. Add pecans. Cook and stir for 2 minutes. Add sugar. Cook and stir for 2 minutes more. Slice off one end of brie so the top is exposed. Spread praline mixture on top. Transfer brie to a baking sheet. Cover loosely with foil. Bake until cheese is partially melted, about 5 minutes. Serve warm.

Politically Correct Mushroom Pâté

~

MAKES 1 HEAPING CUP / PREPARATION TIME: 30 MINUTES

There's no meat in this spread to offend vegetarians, but the meaty flavor of the mushrooms should satisfy any carnivore. This recipe can be prepared the day before a party and served with crackers or toast points.

> *4 tablespoons (1/2 stick) unsalted butter or margarine,*
>   *room temperature*
> *8 ounces mushrooms (button, cremini, shiitake or*
>   *combination), finely chopped*
> *2 teaspoons Worcestershire sauce*
> *1 to 3 teaspoons minced garlic*
> *1/4 cup finely chopped scallions, white parts only (reserve tops)*
> *1/3 cup canned chicken broth or vegetable broth*
> *4 ounces light cream cheese, at room temperature*
> *2 tablespoons minced scallion tops or minced fresh chives*
> *salt and freshly ground black pepper to taste*
> *minced scallion tops or fresh chives for garnish (optional)*

In a medium skillet, over medium-high heat, melt 2 tablespoons butter. Add mushrooms and Worcestershire sauce. Sauté for 3 minutes. Add garlic and scallions. Sauté for 1 minute. Add broth. Cook over high heat until all liquid has evaporated, about 4 to 5 minutes. Remove mushroom mixture from heat and allow to come to room temperature. In a medium bowl, combine cream cheese and remaining 2 tablespoons butter. Stir to mix well. Add the mushroom mixture, scallion tops, salt and pepper. Mix well. Fill a crockery bowl, small casserole dish or soufflé dish with the mushroom mixture. Cover and refrigerate until ready to serve. Bring to room temperature before serving. Garnish with scallion tops or fresh chives.

Coeur à la Crème

~

MAKES ABOUT 3 CUPS / PREPARATION TIME: 20 MINUTES
CHILLING TIME: 12 HOURS

What makes this light, velvety-textured spread so special is the heart-shaped mold in which it's made. The name is French for "heart with cream." Available at cookware shops, the molds are either wicker or ceramic, with holes in the bottom to allow the whey to drain. Traditionally it is served plain with fresh fruit, as a light dessert — but it has savory uses, too. Mix fresh herbs into the cheese, top it with caviar or pesto, or — my favorite — spread it with red pepper jelly and serve with crackers.

8 ounces cream cheese, at room temperature
2 cups (1 pint) cottage cheese, pressed through a fine sieve
1 cup whipping cream, whipped

In a medium bowl, with an electric mixer, whip cream cheese. Beat in cottage cheese until smooth. (Or process cheeses in a food processor until smooth.) Fold whipped cream into cheese mixture. Line a large *coeur à la crème* mold or heart-shaped cake pan pierced with holes with 2 layers of dampened cheesecloth, extending enough beyond edges to overlap filled mold. Fill with cheese mixture. Fold cheesecloth over top. Set mold on rack over a pan (or support strainer on rim of a large, deep bowl). Refrigerate and let drain at least 12 hours. To serve, pull back cheesecloth, invert mold onto serving platter and remove cheesecloth.

Skinny Dips

~

Skimming the fat from traditional dip recipes is no longer a challenge; for all the major fattening ingredients — mayonnaise, cream cheese, sour cream — there are lowfat and nonfat substitutes. These days I instinctively buy the lighter versions whenever a recipe calls for those ingredients (though products that have had all the fat removed from them, I must admit, still don't fool my taste buds), and in any of these recipes you can do the same. Or you can modify your recipes by using as the creamy substance yogurt cheese (find out how to make it on page 57), tofu or cottage cheese blended with a little buttermilk or yogurt. Pureed starchy vegetables such as beans and potatoes also make a far healthier, and surprisingly satisfying, dip base. And then, of course, there are salsas — naturally low in fat but loaded with vibrant flavors that make you forget you're eating healthy.

This chapter is filled with dips in which fat plays a minor role, if any at all. Many, in fact, are actually good for you. Look for others that fit this bill throughout the book, but most notably in the "Worldly Dips" chapter, where you'll not only find classic red and green salsas, but also the Greek tzatziki (yogurt-cucumber dip), Asian eggplant dip and more.

Creamy Lemon-Dill Dip

~

MAKES 1 1/2 CUPS / PREPARATION TIME: 5 MINUTES

The flavors of this almost fat-free dip and suggested dippers were inspired by Scandinavian salads and *smorrebrod*: open-faced sandwiches artistically composed of thinly sliced vegetables, seafoods and meats. Dill and horseradish heighten the flavor of the lemon yogurt-based dip, which pairs beautifully with shrimp, pickled beet slices (drained and blotted dry with paper towels), cauliflower, Belgian endive, radishes, sweet pickles and string beans. A hollowed-out purple cabbage would make a perfect dip bowl.

16 ounces lemon yogurt
1 tablespoon prepared horseradish
1/3 cup finely chopped fresh dill
salt and pepper to taste
fresh dill sprigs for garnish (optional)

In a small, nonreactive bowl, combine yogurt, horseradish and dill. Stir until well blended. Add salt and pepper. Cover and refrigerate. Garnish with fresh dill sprigs. Serve cold.

Chutney Yogurt Dip

~

MAKES ABOUT 2 CUPS / PREPARATION TIME: 10 MINUTES
DRAINING TIME: 8 TO 12 HOURS / CHILLING TIME: 3 HOURS

Using yogurt cheese as a base gives this dip a fresher, lighter taste that's more appealing than the fattening version with cream cheese. The nuts do add some fat; skip them if you're on a strict diet. Serve with rye crackers, lahvosh wafers, carrots, summer squash, etc.

16 ounces plain nonfat yogurt (without gelatin)
4 1/2 ounces mango chutney, finely chopped
1/2 cup chopped scallions
1/2 cup chopped pecans
scallion brush for garnish

To make yogurt cheese: Place yogurt in a strainer lined with a coffee filter or several layers of cheesecloth. Place over a small bowl and cover with plastic wrap. Refrigerate for 8 to 12 hours. The whey will drain off and reduce yogurt by about one third.

To make the dip: Combine yogurt cheese, chutney, scallions and pecans. Cover and refrigerate for at least 3 hours to allow the flavors to blend. Serve cold.

To garnish with scallion brush: Cut off most of white part of scallion and cut off green tops, leaving a 3- to 4-inch piece. With scissors or a sharp knife, cut from top about halfway down the remaining scallion into lengthwise narrow strips. Hold in ice water for 1 to 2 hours until the strips begin to curl.

Mediterranean Salsa with Fresh and Sun-dried Tomatoes

~

MAKES 2 CUPS / PREPARATION TIME: 15 MINUTES

Salsa need not be limited to Mexican ingredients, as this fusion of Southern Italian and South-of-the-border flavors proves. Instead of tortilla chips, scoop up this dazzling mixture with toasted French baguette slices, pita chips, bagel chips or — if you don't mind a few extra calories — polenta chips (page 11).

2 cloves garlic, peeled
1 jalapeño pepper, stemmed, seeded and halved
1/3 cup dried tomatoes packed in oil, drained
  (or reconstituted dry-pack sun-dried tomatoes)
1 to 2 tablespoons olive oil (may use oil from sun-dried tomatoes jar)
1/4 cup chopped fresh basil leaves
1 tablespoon balsamic or red wine vinegar
salt and pepper to taste
pinch of sugar
1/4 cup chopped onion
5 to 6 Roma or plum tomatoes, diced
fresh basil sprigs for garnish (optional)

In a food processor, with the machine running, drop garlic and jalapeño through the chute. Process until finely minced. Add sun-dried tomatoes, olive oil, basil leaves, vinegar, salt, pepper and sugar. Pulse until ingredients are chopped, but not pureed. Add onion and tomatoes. Process until finely diced but still somewhat chunky. Cover and refrigerate until ready to serve. Garnish with fresh basil sprigs.

Watermelon Salsa

MAKES 2 1/2 CUPS / PREPARATION TIME: 20 MINUTES
CHILLING TIME: 1 TO 2 HOURS

This spicy-sweet salsa makes creative use of one of summer's favorite fruits, and it's terrific not only on a tortilla chip but also as a relish for seafood or chicken.

2 cups seeded and finely chopped watermelon
2 tablespoons finely chopped onion
1/4 cup finely chopped water chestnuts
1 to 2 jalapeño peppers, finely chopped
2 tablespoons balsamic vinegar
1/4 teaspoon salt
hot pepper flowers for garnish
  (optional, instructions follow)

In a medium bowl, combine all ingredients except garnish. Cover and refrigerate for 1 to 2 hours. Serve cold. Garnish with hot pepper flower, if desired.

To make hot pepper flowers: For thin-skinned peppers (such as serranos), hold by stem and cut off tips. With scissors or a sharp knife, make 5 cuts a little over half-way to stem. For thicker-skinned peppers (such as jalapeños), cut off tips. Using a sharp knife, make V-shaped cuts around the edge. Hold peppers in ice water 1 to 2 hours until the strips begin to curl.

Honey-Curry Dip

~

MAKES 1 CUP / PREPARATION TIME: 5 MINUTES
STANDING TIME: 30 MINUTES TO OVERNIGHT

Heated together, honey and curry make a warm, spicy, fat-free dip that's great with fruits and vegetables, especially apples and carrots. Also try it with grilled, skewered chicken, scallops and shrimp. For a creamy dip, stir in lowfat or fat-free mayonnaise to taste.

1 cup honey
2 tablespoons curry powder

In a microwave-safe bowl, combine ingredients. In a microwave oven, set on HIGH, cook for 30 seconds. Stir and heat in 30-second increments until honey begins to simmer. Remove from microwave oven. Cover and let stand for 30 minutes to overnight. Serve warm or at room temperature.

Baked Potato Dip

~

MAKES 1 3/4 CUPS / PREPARATION TIME: 15 MINUTES
CHILLING TIME: 30 MINUTES

It may sound strange, but trust me — mashed potatoes makes an excellent, naturally creamy substitute for mayonnaise and cream cheese in dips. This one has the flavors of an overstuffed baked potato, perfect for heaping onto potato skins (page 30), lowfat potato chips or vegetables such as broccoli, pickled Brussels sprouts or green beans.

1 cup cooked mashed potatoes
1/4 cup lowfat sour cream
1/2 cup milk
1 tablespoon fresh minced chives

1/4 teaspoon salt
1/4 teaspoon ground white pepper
fresh chives, chive blossoms for garnish
(optional)

In a medium bowl, combine all ingredients except for garnish. With a wire whisk, whip until smooth. Cover and refrigerate for 30 minutes. Garnish with chives and chive blossoms. Serve cold.

Lightened Aïoli

~

MAKES 2 1/2 CUPS / PREPARATION TIME: 10 MINUTES
CHILLING TIME: 1 HOUR

This dip tastes similar to aïoli, the classic garlic mayonnaise sauce from France which is sometimes thickened with bread crumbs or mashed potatoes. Use with the same dippers you would with traditional aïoli (page 89).

2 cups cooked mashed potatoes
6 cloves garlic, chopped (or more, to taste)
salt to taste
1/4 cup olive oil
1/4 cup herb vinegar
1/4 cup water
fresh parsley for garnish (optional)

In a food processor or blender, combine potatoes, garlic and salt. Puree. With the machine running, gradually add oil, vinegar and water. Process until smooth. Transfer to a serving bowl. Cover and refrigerate for 1 hour before serving to allow flavors to blend. Garnish with parsley. Serve cold or at room temperature.

Lentil Pâté

~

MAKES 4 CUPS / PREPARATION TIME: 1 HOUR
STANDING TIME: 30 MINUTES

Though the word "pâté" generally refers to meat spreads, we take some creative license in applying it to similarly textured herbivorous spreads like this one. Like beans, pureed lentils also makes a versatile dip base. Indian spices flavor this one. Serve with apple slices, green peppers, pita bread or pappadams (page 83).

3/4 cup lentils
1/2 cup brown rice
1 bay leaf
3 1/2 cups water
2 teaspoons olive oil
1 onion, chopped
2 cloves garlic, finely chopped
1 apple, peeled, cored and chopped
2 teaspoons cider vinegar

2 teaspoons curry powder
2 teaspoons ground cumin
1 teaspoon dried oregano
1 teaspoon ground coriander
1/2 teaspoon dry mustard
1/2 teaspoon salt
1/8 teaspoon ground red pepper
apple slices, bay leaves for garnish
  (optional)

In a medium saucepan, combine lentils, rice, bay leaf and water. Bring to a boil. Lower the heat to a simmer, cover the pan and cook for 45 minutes. Discard the bay leaf. Meanwhile, in a nonstick skillet, over medium heat, sauté in the olive oil the onion, garlic and apples until apples are soft and onions are transparent. In a food processor, combine all ingredients. Process to a thick paste, adding a little water if necessary for consistency. Let stand for 30 minutes to 1 hour before serving to allow flavors to meld. Garnish with apple slices and bay leaves. Serve at room temperature.

Roasted Carrot Dip

~

MAKES 2 CUPS / PREPARATION TIME: 1 HOUR, 15 MINUTES
STANDING TIME: 30 MINUTES / CHILLING TIME: OVERNIGHT

Oven-roasting vegetables is a wonderful way to bring out their natural sweetness and is the secret behind this vibrant, full-flavored dip. It also makes a delectable side dish. Dip with pita, wheat crackers or bell peppers.

2 pounds carrots, peeled
3 cloves garlic
3 to 5 tablespoons olive oil, divided
1 teaspoon paprika
1 teaspoon ground ginger
1/4 teaspoon black pepper
2 tablespoons fresh lemon juice
lemon slices for garnish (optional)

Preheat oven to 375 degrees. In a roasting pan, combine carrots and garlic, and coat with 1 tablespoon olive oil. Roast until soft and slightly brown, about 45 minutes to 1 hour. Remove pan from oven to cool. Squeeze garlic from the skins. Place in a food processor. Add carrots, 2 more tablespoons of the olive oil, the paprika, ginger, pepper and lemon juice. Adjust olive oil if desired. Puree. Let stand for 30 minutes. Garnish with lemon slices. Serve warm or cover and refrigerate overnight.

Todd's Carolina Peach Salsa

~

MAKES 2 1/2 CUPS / PREPARATION TIME: 30 MINUTES
CHILLING TIME: 1 HOUR

Charlotte, North Carolina, caterer Todd Townsend has a thing for homegrown peaches, and likes to devise new uses for them. This recipe, he says, has been so well-received that he makes big batches of it every summer as soon as the first local peaches hit the farmers market. He serves it with his homemade pita chips and flour tortilla chips (see below).

6 large, ripe peaches (peeled and cubed)
  or 4 cups frozen peaches (thawed and drained)
1/4 cup minced red onion
2 tablespoons light olive oil
2 to 3 tablespoons freshly squeezed lime juice
zest from 1 lime (the colored part of peel)
2 tablespoons chopped fresh cilantro
1 tablespoon minced garlic
1 1/2 tablespoons rice wine vinegar
1 teaspoon ground cumin
2 fresh jalapeño peppers, seeded and minced
salt and freshly ground black pepper to taste

In a medium nonreactive bowl, combine ingredients. Mash lightly with a fork so mixture is still chunky. Cover and refrigerate for at least 1 hour to blend flavors. Serve cold.

To make your own Tortilla Chips and Pita Chips: Cut flour tortillas and pita bread into triangles. Roll pita bread flat with rolling pin to produce a thin chip. Fry chips in hot vegetable oil until crisp. Pat dry with a paper towel. For lowfat versions of these chips, bake the triangles in a 350-degree oven until crisp, about 6 to 10 minutes.

Spicy Beet and Horseradish Dip

~

MAKES ABOUT 3 1/2 CUPS / PREPARATION TIME: 15 MINUTES

This tangy, shocking-pink dip is virtually void of fat if nonfat sour cream and yogurt are used as the base. For dippers, consider cucumber slices, pita chips, rye or pumpernickel crackers.

1 cup jarred whole pickled beets, drained,
blotted dry and grated by hand
1 1/2 teaspoons prepared horseradish
1 teaspoon spicy brown mustard
2 teaspoons finely chopped chives
2 teaspoons sugar
1/2 teaspoon salt
4 tablespoons rice vinegar
1 cup lowfat or nonfat sour cream
1 cup plain yogurt
fresh parsley for garnish (optional)

In a medium bowl, combine beets, horseradish, mustard, chives, sugar, salt and vinegar. Fold in sour cream and yogurt. Cover and refrigerate. Garnish with fresh parsley. Serve cold.

Surimi Spread

~

MAKES 2 CUPS / PREPARATION TIME: 15 MINUTES
CHILLING TIME: AT LEAST 4 HOURS

The only potentially fattening ingredient in this recipe is the sour cream, and if you use the lowfat or nonfat equivalent, even that's not an issue. You can, of course, use real crab instead of surimi (a crab-flavored, seafood-based substitute), but the latter works so well here that it's tough to justify the extra expense. Serve with melba toast, lahvosh and crackers.

1/2 cup lowfat sour cream
8 or 9 ounces coarsely chopped surimi (crab substitute)
1 tablespoon minced onion
1 tablespoon ketchup
1 teaspoon Worcestershire sauce
1/2 teaspoon lemon juice
1 teaspoon prepared horseradish
1 clove garlic, minced
1/8 teaspoon Old Bay seasoning

In a medium bowl, combine ingredients. Cover and refrigerate for at least 4 hours before serving.

Salmon and White Bean Dip

~

MAKES ABOUT 2 1/2 CUPS / PREPARATION TIME: 10 MINUTES
CHILLING TIME: 30 MINUTES

Using canned white beans as a base, you can make this rich-tasting dip without any additional fat. Serve it with pita bread, toast triangles, lahvosh, cucumbers or celery. Or spread it on a bagel or sandwich.

1 garlic clove, peeled
1 15-ounce can white beans (Great Northern, cannellini, etc.),
  rinsed and drained
1 14 3/4-ounce can salmon, drained
2 tablespoons lemon juice
2 tablespoons fresh dill (or 2 teaspoons dried)
few drops Liquid Smoke (optional)
lemon twist, fresh dill sprigs for garnish (optional)

In a food processor, with machine running, drop garlic through the chute to mince. Add remaining ingredients. Puree until smooth. Cover and refrigerate until ready to serve. Garnish with a lemon twist and fresh dill sprigs.

Roasted Yellow Pepper Dip

~

MAKES ABOUT 1 1/4 CUPS / PREPARATION TIME: 30 MINUTES
CHILLING TIME: 1 HOUR

Enhanced with Southwest seasonings, roasted yellow peppers make a flavorful, golden dip base for this creation of John Wilson, food and beverage director for Fernbank Museum of Natural History in Atlanta. It needs but a smidgen of mayonnaise (lowfat or nonfat are fine) to give it some body. Serve with crackers, pita chips, jicama sticks or other raw vegetables.

nonstick vegetable spray
1/4 cup chopped yellow onion
1 clove garlic, minced
2 large or (3 medium) yellow bell peppers,
  roasted (page 11), stemmed, peeled, seeded
  and coarsely chopped
1 tablespoon chopped fresh basil
1/2 teaspoon ground cumin
1/4 teaspoon chili powder
2 to 3 tablespoons lowfat mayonnaise
salt and pepper to taste
fresh basil leaves for garnish (optional)

Coat a medium skillet with vegetable spray. Place pan over medium heat. Add onions and garlic. Sauté until soft. In a food processor, combine all ingredients except garnish. Process until smooth. Adjust salt and pepper. Transfer to a serving bowl. Cover and refrigerate. Garnish with fresh basil leaves. Serve cold.

Tofu Caesar Dip

~

MAKES 1 1/2 CUPS / PREPARATION TIME: 15 MINUTES
CHILLING TIME: 1 HOUR

Don't let prejudices against tofu keep you from trying it in a dip. In both of these recipes, its spongy texture turns to a smooth, mayonnaise-like consistency, and its bland flavor takes on the tastes of the assertive ingredients it's blended with. Though not lowfat, tofu is leaner than mayonnaise, and offers protein and other nutrients you won't find in "light" substitutes. For the first recipe, we suggest serving as dippers crisp Romaine lettuce leaves and large croutons (page 90) in keeping with the Caesar theme, although it would also be delicious with cherry tomatoes, other raw vegetables — even tortellini.

8 ounces firm tofu, drained
3 tablespoons lemon juice
2 teaspoons Dijon mustard
3 cloves garlic, finely chopped
2 teaspoons anchovy paste
2 to 4 tablespoons olive oil
1/4 cup (1 ounce) finely grated Parmesan cheese

In a food processor, combine tofu, lemon juice, mustard, garlic and anchovy paste. Puree until smooth. With the machine running, slowly add olive oil through the chute. Transfer to a serving bowl. Stir in the Parmesan cheese. Cover and refrigerate. Serve cold.

Soy-Orange Tofu Dip

~

MAKES ABOUT 2 1/2 CUPS / PREPARATION TIME: 15 MINUTES

Asian flavors also succeed in taking the bland out of tofu; the addition of water chestnuts adds crunch without calories.

2 cloves garlic, peeled
1 tablespoon minced fresh ginger
3 tablespoons soy sauce
2 tablespoons orange juice
1 tablespoon grated orange zest (colored part of peel)
1 tablespoon dark sesame oil
1 tablespoon rice wine vinegar
16 ounces firm tofu, drained
1 6-ounce can water chestnuts, drained
1/4 cup sliced scallions
1/4 teaspoon hot chili oil (or to taste)

In a food processor, with machine running, drop garlic cloves through the chute and process until finely minced. Add ginger, soy sauce, orange juice, orange zest, sesame oil, rice wine vinegar and tofu. Process until smooth. Add water chestnuts and scallions. Process just until well blended. Season with hot chili oil. Transfer to a serving bowl. Cover and refrigerate. Serve cold.

Vidalia Onion and Olive Salsa

~

MAKES 2 CUPS / PREPARATION TIME: 20 MINUTES
CHILLING TIME: 4 HOURS

Mild, sweet Vidalia onions are prized in relishes and hosts of other dishes. This dip, in fact, could double as a relish. Dig in with tortilla chips, pita bread, water biscuits or matzoh.

1 medium Vidalia or other mild onion, finely chopped
1 2 1/4-ounce can chopped black olives
2 jalapeño peppers, stemmed, seeded and finely chopped
2 to 4 tablespoons olive oil
1 tablespoon red wine vinegar
1 teaspoon Worcestershire sauce
1 large tomato, finely chopped
1/4 cup finely chopped fresh parsley
dash of hot pepper sauce
salt and black pepper to taste

In a medium nonreactive bowl, combine ingredients. Cover and refrigerate for 4 hours to allow flavors to blend. Taste and adjust seasonings. Serve cold.

Onion-Caper Dip

~

MAKES 2 CUPS / PREPARATION TIME: 15 MINUTES

Assertive flavors wake up the taste of bland cottage cheese in this dip. If you like the texture of cottage cheese, simply stir the ingredients together. But if you prefer a smoother dip, whirl the cottage cheese and buttermilk in a blender to make a sour cream-like base. Good with raw vegetables, sesame crackers, onion crackers.

2 cups lowfat cottage cheese
1/2 cup buttermilk
2 tablespoons grated onion
salt and ground red pepper to taste
3 tablespoons capers, drained
2 cloves garlic, mashed
2 tablespoons lemon juice or lime juice

In a medium bowl, combine ingredients. Cover and refrigerate until ready to use. Serve cold.

New South Caviar

~

Every state in the South, it seems, claims a similar recipe. The longer this one sits, the better the flavor. Heap it on lowfat chips or serve it as a side-dish salad.

3 15-ounce cans black-eyed peas, drained and rinsed
  (or 4 to 5 cups, cooked and drained)
1 small red onion, minced
3 cloves garlic, peeled and minced
1/2 cup olive oil
1/4 cup red wine vinegar
2 teaspoons dried basil
1 teaspoon dried oregano
1/2 teaspoon dried red pepper flakes
1/2 teaspoon salt
1/2 teaspoon freshly ground black pepper

In a medium bowl, combine ingredients. Cover and refrigerate for 2 days or up to 2 weeks. Serve cold.

Worldly Dips

~

Dipping isn't just an American pastime; other cultures have been doing it for centuries, but usually without the cream cheese and mayonnaise essential to so many of our party standbys. Often the creamy constituent is some kind of cooked, dried bean, stale bread or pureed vegetable such as roast eggplant; many would in fact fit just as easily in the "Skinny Dips" chapter. Middle Eastern cultures boast of a particularly strong dip selection, which isn't surprising when you consider that one of the world's best dippers — pita — is part of their daily diet. The chickpea spread hummus and eggplant-tahini puree baba ghanoush are almost as popular in this country nowadays as in their native land. Mexican guacamole and salsa are also so much a part of the American mainstream that we don't even think of them as exotic anymore. We've included them in this chapter anyway, along with some less familiar dips from across the globe. It should be noted, though, that some are traditionally served as salads or condiments — but they all easily adapt to our communal bowl.

Baba Ghanoush

~

2 1/2 CUPS / PREPARATION TIME: 1 HOUR, 20 MINUTES

after-work meal for me has consisted of these two Middle Eastern classics
from a health food store, along with a bag of pita bread. If I have a little more
my own; these are my favorite formulas for each.

1 large eggplant
1/3 cup tahini (sesame paste)
1/4 cup fresh lemon juice
2 cloves garlic, crushed
1 teaspoon ground coriander
salt, black pepper and ground red pepper to taste
2 to 3 tablespoons olive oil (or more, to taste)
minced fresh parsley for garnish (optional)

Preheat oven to 350 degrees. Prick the eggplant in several places with a fork. Place on a baking sheet. Bake for about 1 hour, until very soft. Remove from oven and let cool. Cut eggplant in half, scrape flesh into a medium bowl and discard the skin. Mash the eggplant with
the tahini. Stir in lemon juice, garlic, coriander, salt and peppers. (This may be done in a
food processor.) Stir in olive oil. Cover and refrigerate until ready to serve. Drizzle with more
olive oil, if desired, and garnish with parsley.

Cumin-scented Hummus

MAKES 2 CUPS / PREPARATION TIME: 15 MINUTES

2 large cloves garlic, peeled
1/3 cup tahini (sesame paste)
3 tablespoons lemon juice
1 19-ounce can chickpeas,
  rinsed and drained

1/3 cup water
1 teaspoon ground cumin
salt to taste
1 tablespoon olive oil
paprika for garnish (optional)

In a food processor, with the machine running, drop the garlic cloves through the chute. Process until finely minced. Stir tahini thoroughly to a smooth paste. Add tahini and lemon juice to the processor. Puree to a smooth paste. Add chickpeas and water. Process until very smooth and fluffy. Add cumin and salt. Transfer mixture to a medium serving bowl. Pour a thin film of olive oil on the surface. Swirl the olive oil into the hummus gently with the tip of a knife. Garnish with paprika. Serve at room temperature.

Mexican Guacamole

MAKES 2 CUPS / PREPARATION TIME: 20 MINUTES / CHILLING TIME: AT LEAST 2 HOURS

You can use a food processor to make guacamole, but a fork works better — the avocado should be a little chunky. Add to the avocado the ingredients in the recipe below and you'll have a dip that's much like the one Mexicans like to dip warm tortillas into before a meal.

3 California avocados, peeled, seeded and mashed
1/2 cup finely chopped onion

1/4 cup finely chopped cilantro
1 teaspoon minced garlic (or more, to taste)
1 teaspoon hot pepper sauce (or more, to taste)
salt and black pepper to taste
juice of 1 lime or lemon
finely chopped tomatoes, jalapeño peppers
  and cilantro for garnish (optional)

In a medium bowl, combine ingredients except for garnishes. Mash with a fork until slightly chunky. Cover and refrigerate for at least 2 hours to blend flavors. Garnish as desired.

Tropical Fruit Guacamole

~

MAKES 2 CUPS / PREPARATION TIME: 25 MINUTES
CHILLING TIME: 2 HOURS

Or, you can transplant this concept to the Caribbean and combine the buttery fruit with other tropical fruits and flavors.

1 avocado, peeled and diced
1 mango, peeled and diced
1 papaya, peeled, seeded and diced
1 cup diced red onion
1 jalapeño pepper, seeded and finely chopped
2 tablespoons lime juice

1/4 teaspoon lime zest (colored part of peel)
2 tablespoons chopped cilantro
1/2 teaspoon Pickapeppa sauce
1/4 teaspoon salt
1/2 teaspoon ground white pepper
cilantro for garnish (optional)

In a food processor, combine ingredients. Pulse until slightly chunky. Do not puree. Serve immediately or cover and refrigerate for 2 hours. Garnish with cilantro.

Red Salsa

~

MAKES 1 1/2 CUPS / PREPARATION TIME: 25 MINUTES
CHILLING TIME: 2 HOURS TO OVERNIGHT

Most of us don't even think about making salsa from scratch; sales of the bottled versions, after all, have shot past ketchup. But if you've got a garden full of ripe tomatoes and a half-hour to spend in the kitchen, you should reconsider. Even if made with canned tomatoes, this version is vastly superior to what you can buy.

1 pound tomatoes, coarsely chopped
1/2 cup coarsely chopped scallions
1 jalapeño pepper, finely chopped
3 cloves garlic, finely chopped
1 teaspoon ground cumin
1/3 cup chopped fresh cilantro
2 tablespoons red wine vinegar
1/4 teaspoon ground red pepper
1/4 teaspoon paprika
1/2 teaspoon sugar
1/2 teaspoon salt

In a food processor, combine ingredients. Pulse until chopped but still chunky. Transfer to a serving bowl. Cover and refrigerate for 2 hours to overnight.

Green Salsa

MAKES 3 CUPS / PREPARATION TIME: 30 MINUTES
CHILLING TIME: 2 HOURS TO OVERNIGHT

Tomatillos are like small green tomatoes with a light, lemony flavor and a thin, parchment-like husk. If you have trouble finding them fresh, canned tomatillos can be found in Latin markets.

3 cups water
1 pound tomatillos, shucked and washed
1 tablespoon cider vinegar
1/2 cup coarsely chopped scallions
1/3 cup coarsely chopped fresh cilantro
1/3 cup coarsely chopped fresh parsley
1 jalapeño pepper, seeded and finely chopped
1 medium cucumber, seeded and coarsely chopped
1/2 green bell pepper, coarsely chopped
3 cloves garlic, finely chopped
2 tablespoons fresh lime juice
1 teaspoon ground cumin
1/2 teaspoon salt
fresh cilantro for garnish (optional)

In a medium saucepan, bring water to a boil. Drop in the tomatillos and cider vinegar. Bring water back to a boil, lower heat to medium-low and simmer for 5 minutes. Drain tomatillos and submerge them in ice water. In a food processor, combine tomatillos with remaining ingredients. Process until thick (do not puree). Transfer to a serving bowl. Cover and refrigerate for 2 hours to overnight. Garnish with fresh cilantro.

Taramasalata

MAKES 1 1/2 CUPS / PREPARATION TIME: 20 MINUTES
SOAKING TIME: 30 MINUTES

The toughest part of reproducing this beloved Greek classic will likely be locating the tarama, the salty mullet roe that provides its characteristic sharp, briny flavor. Greek and
Middle Eastern markets generally carry it, though, and if you're as fond of this smooth, distinc-
tively flavored spread as I am, it will be well worth the trip. Serve this to your more adventur-
ous friends — this is not for the timid.

Incidentally, you don't have to soak the roe first, but be forewarned that it is very salty if you
don't. Dip pita chips, plain crackers and radishes.

> *To make an olive
> flower: cut olive
> lengthwise into
> five strips and
> arrange like flower
> petals on top of
> the spread. Place a
> small sprig of pars-
> ley in the center
> of the petals.*

1/2 cup tarama
4 ounces white bread, crust removed, cubed
1/4 cup milk
2 cloves garlic, peeled
2 tablespoons grated onion
3 tablespoons fresh lemon juice
3/4 to 1 cup olive oil
chopped fresh parsley and Greek olives
*   for garnish (optional)*

In a small bowl, place tarama and water to cover. Let tarama soak for 30 minutes. Drain
through a fine-mesh sieve or cheesecloth, removing as much of the salty liquid as possible.
Set aside. In another small bowl, place bread. Pour in milk and toss, allowing bread to
absorb the milk. In a food processor, with the machine running, drop garlic through the
chute to mince. Add tarama, soaked bread, onion and lemon juice. Process until smooth.
With machine running, pour the olive oil in a thin stream and process until completely
incorporated. Taste; if too sharp, add more olive oil. Transfer to a serving bowl. Garnish
with chopped fresh parsley and Greek olives. Serve immediately.

Tzatziki

~

MAKES ABOUT 1 1/4 CUPS / PREPARATION TIME: 15 MINUTES
DRAINING TIME: 3 HOURS

This popular Greek dish is often served as a salad, but by letting the yogurt drain a little longer, it thickens into a lovely, refreshing dip that tastes far richer than it is — it's hard to believe there's only a tablespoon of oil in the whole recipe. Dip with cherry tomatoes or tomato wedges, bell pepper strips, cucumber slices, artichoke leaves, pita, sesame bread sticks.

2 cups plain yogurt (without gelatin)
1 large cucumber, peeled, halved, seeded and grated
1 teaspoon salt
1 tablespoon fresh lemon juice
1 tablespoon olive oil
3 cloves garlic, minced
white pepper to taste
2 tablespoons chopped fresh mint
  or parsley leaves (optional)
fresh mint or parsley leaves, lemon peel
  for garnish (optional)

Place yogurt in a strainer lined with a coffee filter or several layers of cheesecloth. Place over a small bowl and cover with plastic wrap, allowing the whey to drain. Refrigerate for about 3 hours (the longer it drains, the thicker it will be). Meanwhile, in another strainer or colander, place cucumber, sprinkle with salt and let stand over the sink to drain, about 1 hour. Place cucumber on a tea towel, fold over and press out as much of the water as possible. In a medium bowl, mix the yogurt with lemon juice, olive oil, garlic and white pepper to taste. Cover and refrigerate until ready to serve. Just before serving, fold in the cucumber and mint or parsley. Garnish with fresh mint, parsley leaves or lemon peel. Serve cold.

Indian Raita Dip

~

MAKES 1 1/2 CUPS / PREPARATION TIME: 15 MINUTES
DRAINING TIME: 3 HOURS / CHILLING TIME: 1 HOUR TO OVERNIGHT

Similar to tzatziki, this refreshing, yogurt-based dip is traditionally served as a cooling accompaniment to fiery curry dishes. As a dip, it's especially good with a spicy dipper, such as the paper-thin spiced wafers called pappadams found in Indian markets. When deep-fried, they puff up, but they are also good popped into a toaster oven just long enough for them to crisp up. Or, try the Curry Crackers suggested below.

2 cups plain yogurt (without gelatin)
1 medium cucumber, peeled, seeded and finely diced
1/2 teaspoon salt
1 scallion, finely sliced
2 Roma tomatoes, finely diced
fresh mint leaves, chili powder for garnish (optional)

Strain yogurt to make yogurt cheese as in preceding tzatziki recipe. Meanwhile, combine cucumber and salt, and drain it in the same manner for 1 hour. In a medium bowl, combine yogurt cheese, cucumber, scallion and tomatoes. Cover and refrigerate for 1 hour or overnight. Garnish with mint leaves and chili powder.

Curry Crackers: In a small saucepan, melt 2 tablespoons of butter with 2 teaspoons curry powder and 1/4 teaspoon cumin. Brush on plain, thin crackers such as Bremner and toast under a broiler until lightly browned, 1 to 2 minutes. Watch very carefully; they burn easily. Makes 1 to 2 dozen.

White Bean Skordalia

~

MAKES 4 CUPS / PREPARATION TIME: 25 MINUTES
STANDING TIME: 30 MINUTES / CHILLING TIME: OVERNIGHT

Almonds, walnuts, bread crumbs, potatoes, white beans, mayonnaise — these ingredients and various combinations of them have all gone into this popular Greek garlic spread. I particularly like this version because it's considerably less fatty than the typical olive oil-laden recipes. It owes its creaminess instead to pureed white beans and bread crumbs. Serve with pita triangles or thin baguette slices brushed with olive oil, sprinkled with crumbled oregano and baked.

2 cups cubed day-old French bread, crust removed
1 19-ounce can cannellini beans, rinsed and drained
1 teaspoon salt
3 cloves garlic, coarsely chopped
1/2 teaspoon ground black pepper
1 tablespoon fresh lemon juice
2 tablespoons olive oil
1/2 cup water
crushed black pepper, lemon slices for garnish (optional)

In a food processor, place bread cubes. Process into coarse crumbs. Add beans, salt, garlic, pepper and lemon juice. Blend until almost smooth. With the machine running, pour in olive oil and water. Blend to incorporate. Transfer to a serving bowl. Let stand at least 30 minutes to allow flavors to blend, or cover and refrigerate overnight. Garnish with crushed black pepper and lemon slices.

Spicy Peanut Satay Dip

~

MAKES 1 1/2 CUPS / PREPARATION TIME: 30 MINUTES

Throughout Southeast Asia, satay sauce is synonymous with dip — skewered, marinated bits of meat are grilled and dunked into a creamy, spicy peanut sauce such as this one. Serve with Chicken Satays (recipe follows) or with raw vegetables. For a terrific shortcut version of this dip, see page 111.

2 tablespoons vegetable oil	*1/2 cup peanut butter*
2 teaspoons sesame oil	*3 tablespoons soy sauce*
3 cloves garlic, finely chopped	*1 tablespoon chopped lemon zest*
1/2 cup finely chopped onion	*(colored part of peel)*
2 tablespoons finely chopped fresh ginger	*1 tablespoon chopped orange zest*
1 teaspoon dried red pepper flakes	*1/2 cup water or chicken stock*

In a medium saucepan, over medium heat, place the vegetable oil and sesame oil. When hot, add garlic and onion and cook for 1 to 2 minutes, until just beginning to soften. Add ginger, red pepper flakes, peanut butter, soy sauce, zests and water. Whisk together until blended. Cook over medium heat for about 5 minutes. Remove from heat. Transfer to a serving bowl. Cover and refrigerate until about 30 minutes before serving. Serve at room temperature.

Chicken Satays: In a medium bowl, marinate 3/4 pound chicken strips in following mixture for 30 minutes to 4 hours: 1/3 cup fresh lemon juice, 1/4 cup soy sauce, 2 teaspoons dark sesame oil, 2 tablespoons vegetable oil, 2 tablespoons minced fresh ginger and 2 minced cloves garlic. Place chicken on skewers and grill or broil for about 10 minutes, turning once, until cooked through.

Tapenade

～

MAKES 1 3/4 CUPS / PREPARATION TIME: 30 MINUTES
CHILLING TIME: 1 TO 2 DAYS

This thick, lusty paste of olives, anchovies, tuna and seasonings comes from France's Provence region and tastes wonderful spread on French bread slices, water biscuits, bell pepper strips and Belgian endive leaves.

2 cloves garlic, finely chopped
1/2 cup finely chopped onion
1 cup pitted imported black olives (such as kalamata)
  finely chopped
1 6-ounce can tuna, drained
2 tablespoons finely chopped fresh parsley
2 tablespoons finely chopped fresh thyme
1 2-ounce tin anchovies, drained and mashed
2 tablespoons lemon juice
1 tablespoon minced lemon zest (colored part of peel)
1/4 cup mayonnaise
freshly ground black pepper to taste
lemon zest, fresh parsley, thyme sprigs for garnish
  (optional)

In a medium bowl, combine ingredients until well blended. This may be done in the food processor, but be careful not to overprocess; the mixture should be thick, not liquefied. Cover and refrigerate, preferably for 1 to 2 days, until 30 minutes before ready to serve. Garnish with lemon zest, fresh parsley and thyme sprigs. Serve at room temperature.

Caponata

MAKES 5 CUPS / PREPARATION TIME: 1 HOUR, 30 MINUTES
STANDING TIME: 1 HOUR / CHILLING TIME: OVERNIGHT TO 4 DAYS

In Sicily, this stewed vegetable dish is served as a relish or side dish. But over here it's a popular hors d'oeuvre, served atop toasted baguette slices, pita chips or melba toast. I like to use it both ways; I might even toss the leftovers with pasta, along with a sprinkle of Parmesan cheese. It makes a lot, but it will keep for several days in the refrigerator and for months in the freezer.

1 large eggplant, peeled, cut into 1/2-inch cubes (about 2 cups)
1 medium zucchini, cut into 1/2-inch cubes (about 1 cup)
1 tablespoon salt
1/4 cup olive oil
1/2 cup chopped onion
1/2 cup chopped red bell pepper
1/2 cup chopped celery
2 teaspoons minced garlic
1 cup chopped tomatoes
1/4 cup pitted and chopped black olives
1 tablespoon capers
2 teaspoons sugar
1 tablespoon balsamic vinegar
parsley, black olives, capers for garnish (optional)

In a colander, place eggplant and zucchini, sprinkle with salt and let drain for 1 hour. Rinse eggplant and zucchini, and pat dry. In a large skillet, heat half the olive oil. Add eggplant and zucchini. Sauté until soft and beginning to brown, 10 to 15 minutes. Add remaining olive oil and the onion, red bell pepper, celery and garlic. Sauté for 15 minutes more. Add tomatoes, olives, capers, sugar and vinegar. Simmer for 30 minutes, stirring occasionally. Transfer to a serving bowl. Cover and refrigerate overnight or up to 4 days. Garnish with parsley, black olives and capers.

Sesame-Ginger Dip

~

MAKES A SCANT 1 CUP / PREPARATION TIME: 10 MINUTES
STANDING TIME: 30 MINUTES TO OVERNIGHT

A dip doesn't have to be thick and gloppy — in Asia it's more likely to take the form of a thin but highly flavorful dipping sauce for egg rolls, spring rolls, sushi or tempura. Try this dip with Asian vegetables — such as baby corn and baby bok choy — as well as shrimp, chicken breast cubes, chicken wings or tempura. Or for something crunchier, try Wonton Bow Ties or Sesame Wonton Chips (recipes follow).

2 tablespoons sesame oil
2 tablespoons toasted sesame seeds
1/2 cup soy sauce
1/2 cup rice vinegar
2 tablespoons minced fresh ginger
2 scallions, thinly sliced

In a serving bowl, combine ingredients. Let stand for 30 minutes before serving. May be refrigerated overnight if scallions are held out until 30 minutes before serving.

Wonton Bow Ties: Preheat oven to 375 degrees. Pinch wonton between the index finger and thumb to form a bow shape. Spray a baking sheet with vegetable oil. Lay the bows on the baking sheet. Spray lightly with oil. Bake until crisp and lightly browned, about 5 to 6 minutes. Store in an airtight container. Bow Ties will keep for 3 to 4 days.

Sesame Wonton Chips: Cut wontons in half diagonally, or leave whole. Brush with egg white, then sprinkle with sesame seeds. Bake as above.

Aïoli

~

MAKES 1 1/4 CUPS / PREPARATION TIME: 10 MINUTES
CHILLING TIME: 3 HOURS TO 2 DAYS

This garlicky mayonnaise is known as the butter of Provence, and is used to sauce fish, smear on bread, flavor bouillabaisse and adorn all types of vegetables. It's especially good with fresh fennel slices, blanched green beans, asparagus and boiled potatoes.

1 large egg
2 tablespoons white wine vinegar
1/4 cup water
2 to 4 cloves garlic, crushed in a garlic press
3/4 cup olive oil
1/2 teaspoon salt

In the top of a double boiler, whisk together the egg, vinegar and water. Cook over simmering water (not boiling), whisking continually, until mixture thickens. Remove the boiler from the heat. Add garlic. Continue whisking and slowly add olive oil until incorporated. Whisk in the salt. Transfer to a serving bowl. Cover tightly and refrigerate for at least 3 hours or up to 2 days.

Gazpacho Dip

~

MAKES 5 CUPS / PREPARATION TIME: 25 MINUTES
CHILLING TIME: 2 HOURS OR OVERNIGHT

Thicken the popular Spanish soup to dipping consistency and what do you get? A Spanish salsa, you might say. It is, incidentally, good creamy as well; simply stir in some sour cream right before serving. Dip Parmesan-Herb Croutons (recipe follows) and tortilla chips.

4 large tomatoes (about 2 pounds), chopped	*1 teaspoon salt*
1 cucumber, peeled and cut into l-inch cubes	*2 tablespoons olive oil*
3 scallions, cut into 1-inch lengths	*2 tablespoons red wine vinegar*
1 green bell pepper, cut into 1-inch squares	*1 tablespoon sherry (optional)*
2 tablespoons coarsely chopped parsley	*1/4 teaspoon hot pepper sauce*
1 tablespoon coarsely chopped basil	*1 teaspoon ground cumin*
1/2 teaspoon paprika	*1 cup toasted bread crumbs*
1/2 teaspoon sugar	

In a food processor, combine all ingredients. Pulse until mixture is finely chopped. (Do not puree.) Cover and refrigerate for 2 hours or overnight to develop flavors.

Parmesan-Herb Croutons: Cut 1 loaf French or Italian bread in 1-inch cubes. (You should have about 6 cups.) Preheat oven to 350 degrees. In a medium bowl, combine bread cubes with 2 tablespoons finely chopped parsley, 2 finely chopped cloves garlic, 2 tablespoons olive oil and 2 tablespoons Parmesan cheese. On a baking sheet, spread mixture. Bake until bread cubes are dry and beginning to brown, about 25 to 30 minutes.

Liptauer Cheese Spread

～

MAKES ABOUT 1 3/4 CUPS / PREPARATION TIME: 20 MINUTES
CHILLING TIME: OVERNIGHT

Named for a province in Hungary, Liptauer is traditionally made from a soft, sheep's milk cheese, but this Americanized version nicely suffices. Spread on rye, wheat and pumpernickel crackers; it's also a natural for radishes and celery.

8 ounces cream cheese, softened
1/2 cup (1 stick) unsalted butter, softened
1/4 cup sour cream
1 1/4 teaspoons paprika
1 tablespoon anchovy paste
1 clove garlic, mashed
2 tablespoons minced fresh chives
  (or 2 teaspoons dried)
2 teaspoons caraway seeds
1/2 teaspoon dry mustard
salt to taste
1/4 teaspoon black pepper

In a medium bowl, with electric mixer, blend cream cheese with butter. Add remaining ingredients and mix well. Transfer to a serving bowl. Cover and refrigerate overnight. Serve cold or at room temperature.

Asian Eggplant Dip

MAKES ABOUT 4 CUPS / PREPARATION TIME: 1 HOUR

Eggplant is one of those vegetable chameleons that, when roasted until soft, can take on myriad flavors. This Asian adaptation has another bonus: It's very low in fat. Scoop with pita chips, shrimp chips, wonton chips or rice crackers.

oil for greasing baking sheet
2 large eggplants, halved lengthwise
1 tablespoon sesame seeds, toasted
1 tablespoon finely chopped fresh ginger
1 1/2 teaspoons Oriental sesame oil
2 tablespoons soy sauce
1 tablespoon sherry
1 tablespoon rice wine vinegar
2 tablespoons hoisin sauce
1 tablespoon oyster sauce

1 1/2 teaspoons Chinese chili paste
2 teaspoons honey
1 tablespoon finely chopped orange zest
    (colored part of peel)
1 tablespoon vegetable oil
3 scallions, finely chopped
2 cloves garlic, finely chopped
2 tablespoons finely chopped cilantro
    (optional)

Preheat oven to 375 degrees. On a lightly greased baking sheet, place eggplants, cut side down. Place in oven and cook until eggplants are soft, 30 to 45 minutes. Remove from oven and set aside to cool. In a small bowl, combine the sesame seeds, ginger, sesame oil, soy sauce, sherry, vinegar, hoisin sauce, oyster sauce, chili paste, honey and orange zest. Whisk together and set aside. When eggplants have cooled, scoop out pulp onto a cutting board and cut into medium-size pieces. In a large skillet, heat the vegetable oil. Add scallions and garlic. Cook until soft but not brown, for 1 to 2 minutes. Add eggplant and seasoning mixture and stir to combine. Cook over medium heat for 2 to 3 minutes to heat through. Transfer to a serving bowl. Fold in cilantro. Serve warm or at room temperature.

Bagna Cauda

~

The name is Italian for "hot bath," referring to the rich, pungent, Piedmont-style fondue into which vegetables are dipped. Belgian endive leaves, blanched and chilled cauliflower, Brussels sprouts, broccoli, green beans, fennel and baby carrots are particularly well-suited. While most versions contain mainly butter, this lavish one is cream based.

2 tablespoons olive oil
2 cloves garlic, finely chopped
1 tablespoon finely chopped lemon zest (colored part of peel)
1 tablespoon finely chopped orange zest
1 1- to 2-ounce tin anchovy fillets, drained and mashed
3 cups heavy cream

In a large, heavy saucepan, heat the oil over medium heat. Add garlic and cook until soft but not brown, 1 to 2 minutes. Stir in lemon zest, orange zest and anchovies. Add cream. Bring to a boil. Reduce heat to medium and cook until reduced by almost half. Transfer to a fondue pot or chafing dish. Serve warm.

Pantry Dips

~

Some of the world's best dishes were invented with whatever happened to be handy, and the same holds true for dips. I call these "pantry dips" because they rely most heavily on pantry items, as well as staple ingredients from the refrigerator: eggs, bacon, dairy products and common vegetables like onion and bell pepper.

Cheap convenience foods like dried soup mix, canned tuna and ready-to-eat pork barbecue are transformed easily into party fare when mixed with cream cheese or sour cream and a few choice flavorings. A well-stocked spice rack, a freezer full of mixed nuts and a selection of interesting condiments ensures that you will always have the makings for an instant hors d'oeuvre to toss together for unexpected company or for a potluck.

Cooked-Egg Mayonnaise Dijon

MAKES ABOUT 2 CUPS / PREPARATION TIME: 25 MINUTES

I used to love to make homemade mayonnaise, until all those scary headlines started appearing about people getting salmonella poisoning from eating raw eggs. So I was thrilled to find in an egg pamphlet this recipe based on one Julia Child developed using cooked eggs. Though not quite as delicate as traditional, it works beautifully — and takes to assertive flavorings like a hefty spoonful of Dijon mustard. Use as a dip for any vegetable, seafood or skewered meat — or spread it on a sandwich. Or for a more basic mayonnaise, reduce the mustard to 1 teaspoon. For some ideas for flavoring mayonnaise, see next page.

2 tablespoons all-purpose flour
1/2 cup water
1 large egg
2 hard-boiled egg yolks
1 tablespoon Dijon mustard
1/2 teaspoon salt, or to taste
1 1/2 teaspoons wine vinegar (or to taste)
1 1/2 teaspoons lemon juice (or to taste)
1 cup olive oil or vegetable oil, or a combination
white pepper to taste

In a saucepan, place flour. Whisking constantly, gradually blend in water until smooth. Whisking slowly and reaching all over the bottom of the pan, bring mixture to a slow boil. Boil for 1 minute, whisking constantly. Remove from heat, break egg into center of mixture and quickly whisk it in. Return sauce to heat and, still whisking, boil slowly for 15 seconds. Transfer to a food processor or blender. Sieve yolks into sauce. Blend until smooth. Add mustard, salt, vinegar and lemon juice. Process several seconds until smooth. With machine running, add olive oil in a thin stream. Add pepper. Taste for seasoning. Add more salt, vinegar and lemon juice if necessary. Transfer to a container or serving bowl. Cover and refrigerate for up to 1 week.

Quick Fixes, Part One

~

Into a cup of mayonnaise, sour cream, softened cream cheese, yogurt cheese or a combination, stir in:

— flavored mustard (green peppercorn, horseradish, honey)

— olivada (olive paste)

— caviar

— corn relish

— freshly grated or bottled horseradish

— tomato paste or sun-dried tomato paste

— freshly grated Parmesan cheese or crumbled blue cheese

— minced fresh garlic, or roasted, pureed garlic

— curry powder

— chopped fresh herbs

— crystallized ginger

— orange, lime or lemon zest

— minced chipotle peppers

— anchovy paste

Curried Bacon-Peanut Dip

~

MAKES 1 1/2 CUPS / PREPARATION TIME: 15 MINUTES

This simple dip is rich, salty and absolutely addictive. Leftovers are great spooned over a steaming baked potato. It's a natural for crackers and potato chips — although given its high sodium content, you may want to go with a less salty dipper. Try it with bell pepper wedges, celery or the Spicy Potato Skins (page 30).

1/2 pound bacon
8 ounces sour cream
1/3 cup chopped peanuts
2 tablespoons milk (or more to thin)
1/2 teaspoon curry powder

In a skillet, fry bacon until crisp. Drain and crumble. In a medium bowl, combine bacon and remaining ingredients. Cover and refrigerate until ready to serve.

Smoked Oyster Dip

~

MAKES 3 CUPS / PREPARATION TIME: 15 MINUTES
CHILLING TIME: 2 HOURS

If you don't normally keep smoked oysters on hand, you might want to after trying this delicious dip. Try it on melba toast.

8 ounces cream cheese
1 1/2 cups mayonnaise
1 3.66-ounce can smoked oysters,
    drained and chopped
1 3 1/4-ounce can black olives, chopped
a few drops hot pepper sauce

In a medium bowl, mix cream cheese and mayonnaise until creamy. Stir in other ingredients. Cover and refrigerate for at least 2 hours before serving.

Sweet Mustard Dip

MAKES ABOUT 3 CUPS / PREPARATION TIME: 15 MINUTES
STANDING TIME: OVERNIGHT / CHILLING TIME: 1 HOUR

This tangy-sweet mustard sauce is a welcome switch from the usual mayonnaise and cream cheese-based dips. Along with most any vegetable — broccoli, cauliflower, Brussels sprouts come to mind — it's good with a variety of skewered meat dippers, such as kielbasa, ham, smoked turkey and chicken nuggets.

1 cup dry mustard
1 cup wine vinegar (red or white)
3 eggs
1 cup sugar

In a medium nonreactive bowl, mix mustard and vinegar. Let stand, covered, overnight at room temperature. In the top of a double boiler, over boiling water, mix eggs with sugar. Stir in mustard mixture. Cook, stirring constantly, until smooth and thickened. Transfer to a serving bowl. Cover and refrigerate for 1 hour.

Jezebel Sauce

~

MAKES 3 1/2 CUPS / PREPARATION TIME: 5 MINUTES

Versions of this spicy-sweet, sinus-clearing sauce have made their way into Junior League and community cookbooks everywhere. And no wonder: it's extremely easy, different and versatile. Pour the leftovers in pretty jars and you've got a nice gift. If spread over cream cheese, serve with assorted crackers. Or, serve in a bowl as a dipping sauce for sliced kielbasa, skewered ham, chicken nuggets or meatballs.

1 16-ounce jar apple jelly
1 16-ounce jar pineapple preserves
1 4-ounce jar prepared horseradish
1 0.85-ounce container dry mustard
cream cheese for serving (optional)

In a medium bowl, combine ingredients except for cream cheese. Cover and refrigerate indefinitely. Serve over cream cheese, if desired.

Quick Fixes, Part Two

~

Top an 8-ounce package of cream cheese with:

— Pickapeppa sauce

— cocktail sauce topped with baby shrimp or crabmeat

— pesto

— sun-dried tomato bits in oil

— mango or other flavor chutney, chopped peanuts

— hot pepper jelly

— Vidalia onion, chowchow, corn or other relish

— good quality barbecue sauce

— salsa, shredded cheddar cheese

— basil oil or other flavored olive oil

— soy sauce or hoisin sauce, sprinkled with sesame seeds

— orange marmalade, chopped pecans

Note: For a prettier presentation, pack the cream cheese into a small mold or tart pan lined with plastic wrap, chill for several hours and unmold before topping.

Jalapeño Jelly Dip

~

MAKES 3 1/2 CUPS / PREPARATION TIME: 15 MINUTES

This unlikely combination of flavors comes together deliciously in this crunchy, hot/sweet dip. Try it on a water biscuit, banana chips or Wonton Chips (see recipe, 88).

1 cup (about 3 ounces) slivered almonds
1/2 cup shredded coconut
1 pound (2 8-ounce packages) cream cheese, softened
6 ounces green jalapeño jelly

Preheat oven to 325 degrees. On a baking sheet, spread almonds and coconut in a thin layer. Toast in oven until lightly browned, about 8 to 10 minutes. Transfer to a medium bowl. Stir in cream cheese and jalapeno jelly. Cover and refrigerate until ready to serve.

Pepperoncini Spread

~

MAKES 2 CUPS / PREPARATION TIME: 10 MINUTES

Aside from tossing them into salads or antipasto, what do you do with pepperoncini — those tangy, pale-green pickled peppers that appear in every salad bar? Try this intriguing alternative, for dipping with toasted bread, pepperoni, melba toast or Italian bread sticks.

8 ounces cream cheese
1/4 cup sour cream
1/4 cup (1 ounce) grated Parmesan cheese
1/8 teaspoon garlic powder
1 12-ounce jar pepperoncini, drained, stemmed,
   seeded and chopped
1 plum tomato, diced (optional)

In a medium bowl, combine cream cheese, sour cream, Parmesan cheese and garlic powder. Stir until well blended. Stir in pepperoncini and tomato. Mix well. Cover and refrigerate until ready to serve.

Asparagus and Tuna Mousse

~

MAKES ABOUT 8 CUPS / PREPARATION TIME: 25 MINUTES
CHILLING TIME: 5 HOURS

Though initially skeptical, tasters couldn't resist this peculiar mix of convenience foods and refrigerator staples, which, when made in a pretty mold, looks downright glamorous. It's good with crackers, celery and other sturdy raw vegetables.

1 pound (2 8-ounce packages) cream cheese, softened
1 cup mayonnaise
2 6-ounce cans tuna packed in water, drained and crumbled
2 10 3/4-ounce cans asparagus soup, undiluted
2 1/4-ounce envelopes unflavored gelatin
1/2 cup water
1 medium onion, minced
1 medium green bell pepper, minced
vegetable oil or nonstick vegetable spray

In a large bowl, combine cream cheese and mayonnaise. Stir in tuna. In a saucepan, over medium-low heat, heat soup. In another saucepan, soften gelatin in water. Stir over low heat to dissolve. Mix soup and gelatin into cream cheese mixture. Stir in onion and green pepper. In a 2-quart greased glass baking dish or gelatin mold, pour mixture. Cover and refrigerate for 5 hours. When ready to serve, unmold onto a serving plate.

Clamdigger Dip

~

MAKES 1 1/2 CUPS / PREPARATION TIME: 15 MINUTES
CHILLING TIME: 1 HOUR

Clams have been a favorite dip addition probably even longer than dry onion soup mix. Story has it that the day after a clam dip recipe appeared on the Kraft Music Hall television program in the 1950s, there wasn't a can of clams left in New York City.

This is a slight variation on the original, and it has just as much appeal today. Serve with chips and crackers.

1 7 1/2- to 8-ounce can minced clams, drained,
  liquid reserved
8 ounces cream cheese, softened
1 tablespoon lemon juice
1 tablespoon grated onion
1 tablespoon minced parsley
1 teaspoon Worcestershire sauce
salt and hot pepper sauce to taste
fresh parsley sprig, lemon crescent for garnish (optional)

In a medium bowl, combine all ingredients except for clam liquid and garnish, and mix. Cover and refrigerate for at least 1 hour to blend flavors. If too thick, add just enough of the clam liquid to thin to desired consistency. Garnish with fresh parsley sprigs and lemon crescent.

Bloody Mary Dip

~

MAKES 1 1/4 CUPS / PREPARATION TIME: 10 MINUTES
CHILLING TIME: AT LEAST 1 HOUR

The flavors in the classic bar drink marry as well with cream cheese as they do with vodka. The ideal dipper? A celery stick, of course.

8 ounces cream cheese, softened
1/4 cup vegetable juice cocktail
2 teaspoons prepared horseradish
1 teaspoon celery salt
1 teaspoon dried chives
1 teaspoon Worcestershire sauce
black pepper and hot pepper sauce to taste

In a small bowl, beat cream cheese with electric mixer until fluffy. Gradually beat in vegetable juice cocktail. Stir in remaining ingredients. Transfer to a serving bowl. Cover and refrigerate for at least 1 hour.

Homemade French Onion Dip

~

MAKES 1 CUP / PREPARATION TIME: 2 MINUTES
CHILLING TIME: 3 HOURS

When that urge for California Dip and chips strikes, you don't necessarily have to run out and buy a box of onion soup mix. Ida Richardson of Pendleton, South Carolina, devised a recipe for the mix from pantry staples that we found a lot less salty, but just as tasty. And like its commercial counterpart, the dipper possibilities are as endless as your supermarket's produce bin and snack-food aisle.

1 cup sour cream
2 to 4 tablespoons French Onion Dip Mix (recipe follows)

In a small bowl, mix ingredients. Cover and refrigerate for at least 3 hours.

French Onion Dip Mix

~

MAKES 1/2 CUP / PREPARATION TIME: 2 MINUTES

1/2 teaspoon onion powder
1/2 teaspoon salt
1/4 teaspoon sugar
1/4 teaspoon Kitchen Bouquet Browning Sauce
1/2 cup minced dehydrated onion

Mix ingredients until uniformly brown. Cover tightly and store in pantry until ready to use. Keeps indefinitely.

Better-Than-Ranch Buttermilk Dip

~

MAKES 1 CUP / PREPARATION TIME: 5 MINUTES
CHILLING TIME: 1 HOUR

This dip was inspired by the contents of a spice rack. I especially like the subtle Mexican flavor supplied by the cumin. Serve with broccoli, cauliflower, summer squash, jicama, kohlrabi or any other raw vegetable. Or dip chicken wings into it.

1/2 cup buttermilk
1/2 cup mayonnaise
1 teaspoon parsley flakes
1 teaspoon dried chives

1 teaspoon ground cumin
1/2 teaspoon garlic powder
salt and black pepper to taste

In a medium bowl, combine ingredients. Mix with a fork. Cover and refrigerate for 1 hour. Shake or mix before serving.

Barbecue Lover's Dip

~

MAKES 3 1/2 CUPS / PREPARATION TIME: 5 MINUTES

I thank Ellie Hamilton of Hiawassee, Georgia, for sharing this remarkably simple but clever discovery she made while rummaging through her cupboards to come up with a last-minute chip dip to take to a church party. Canned barbecue never tasted so good.

1 10-ounce can pork barbecue
16 ounces sour cream
1 teaspoon Liquid Smoke
1/8 teaspoon ground red pepper

In a large bowl, combine ingredients. Cover and refrigerate until ready to serve.

Easy Black Bean and Corn Dip

~

MAKES 1 1/2 CUPS / PREPARATION TIME: 5 MINUTES
CHILLING TIME: 1 HOUR

Another great-tasting dip so ridiculously easy it is instantly committed to memory. It's also almost fat-free, so long as you stick to fat-free pita chips or tortilla chips.

1 16-ounce can black beans, drained and rinsed
1 9 1/2-ounce jar corn relish
dash of lime juice
few shots of hot pepper sauce (optional)

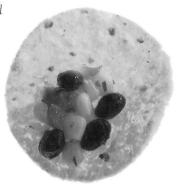

In a medium bowl, combine ingredients. Cover and refrigerate for 1 hour.

Tuna Mountain

MAKES ABOUT 2 1/2 CUPS / PREPARATION TIME: 15 MINUTES
CHILLING TIME: 1 HOUR

No one can keep a straight face when I tell them the name of this rich, smooth, tarragon-flavored spread . . . nor can they keep from going back for more. I got it years ago from Terrace Hill, the Iowa governor's mansion, and it's still one of the best uses for canned tuna I've ever encountered (would this qualify as the only mountain in Iowa?). It's elegant enough to serve at a formal cocktail party. But if you want your guests to take you seriously, you might introduce it as Tuna Pâté instead. Serve with whole radishes, celery, rye bread or crackers.

1 cup (2 sticks) butter or margarine
8 ounces cream cheese
2 6-ounce cans tuna, drained
2 tablespoons minced scallion
1 tablespoon lemon juice
1 tablespoon capers
1/2 teaspoon dried tarragon
salt and pepper to taste
1/4 cup minced parsley
1 hard-boiled egg yolk, sieved,
  for garnish (optional)

With an electric mixer, food processor or blender, cream together butter and cheese. Beat in tuna, scallion, lemon juice, capers, tarragon, salt and pepper until smooth. Transfer to a serving plate and shape into a mountain. Sprinkle parsley around base. Garnish with egg. Cover and refrigerate for 1 hour.

Pantry Peanut Dip

~

MAKES 2 CUPS / PREPARATION TIME: 10 MINUTES
CHILLING TIME: 1 HOUR

The more international your cupboard, the wider your options for spur-of-the-moment entertaining. Here's a fiery, Thai-style pantry version of satay sauce, good for raw **vegeta-bles** as well as the more traditional skewered, grilled meats (see page 85).

1 cup chicken broth
1 cup smooth peanut butter
1/2 cup coconut milk
1 teaspoon fish sauce
1 tablespoon hot garlic chili paste (or to taste)
1 tablespoon dark sesame oil
2 tablespoons packed dark brown sugar
1/4 cup chopped roasted peanuts

In a blender or food processor, combine all ingredients except peanuts. Blend until smooth. Transfer to a serving bowl. Cover and refrigerate for 1 hour. When ready to serve, sprinkle with chopped peanuts.

Lenada's Hospitality Spread

~

MAKES 4 CUPS / PREPARATION TIME: 20 MINUTES
CHILLING TIME: OVERNIGHT

Food consultant Lenada Merrick prescribes this spread to anyone in need of an easy but impressive hors d'oeuvre. For a fancier presentation, she suggests serving it in a scooped-out fresh pineapple half. Cube the fresh pineapple for dipping, or save for another use. Other complementary dippers: sesame crackers, bread sticks, carrot sticks, bell pepper strips, celery sticks.

> *1 pound (2 8-ounce packages) cream cheese,*
> * room temperature*
> *1 8-ounce can crushed pineapple*
> *1 cup chopped pecans*
> *1/4 cup minced green bell pepper*
> *2 tablespoons minced onion*
> *1 teaspoon seasoned salt (or to taste)*

In a medium bowl, with electric mixer, beat cream cheese until soft. Stir in remaining ingredients and mix. Transfer to a serving container. Cover and refrigerate overnight.

Curried Chutney Dip

~

MAKES ABOUT 3 CUPS / PREPARATION TIME: 10 MINUTES

A bottle of mango chutney and a can of curry powder open up all kinds of exotic-tasting dip possibilities. Serve this one with sesame bread sticks or any kind of cracker.

8 ounces cream cheese, softened
2/3 cup sour cream
1/2 cup mango chutney, chopped
1 tablespoon curry powder
dash of garlic powder
1 cup chopped salted cashews

In a medium bowl, mix ingredients. Cover and refrigerate until ready to serve.

Polynesian Ginger Dip

~

MAKES 1 1/4 CUPS / PREPARATION TIME: 10 MINUTES
CHILLING TIME: OVERNIGHT

Chances are, this dip originated not in the tropics but in the 'burbs. Its seasonings do give that mundane mayonnaise-sour cream mixture an island twist, though. Try it with raw vegetables, pineapple chunks, sesame crackers or Wonton Bow Ties (page 88).

1/2 cup mayonnaise
1/2 cup sour cream
2 tablespoons minced parsley
2 tablespoons finely chopped water chestnuts
1 tablespoon finely chopped onion
1 tablespoon finely chopped candied ginger
1 clove garlic, minced
1 1/2 teaspoons soy sauce

In a medium bowl, blend mayonnaise and sour cream. Fold in remaining ingredients. Cover and refrigerate overnight.

Party Bean Dip

~

Layered Mexican dips turn up at every party for good reasons: everyone loves them, they're easy on the cook and they're fun to doctor up. Cold versions may start with a mixture of cream cheese and taco seasoning mix spread on the bottom of a clear pie plate, followed by guacamole, salsa, shredded lettuce, grated cheddar cheese, chopped scallions and sliced pitted black olives. You're more likely to have all the makings for this warm, bean-based version.

> *1 1-pound can refried beans*
> *2 tablespoons taco seasoning mix (from 1 1/4-ounce package)*
> *1 cup sour cream*
> *2 2 1/4-ounce cans sliced black olives, drained*
> *2 medium tomatoes, diced and drained*
> *1 cup sliced scallions (green part only)*

In a small saucepan, over medium heat, heat beans through until smoking. In a 6- to 8-inch-wide serving bowl (preferably clear glass) spread hot mashed beans on the bottom. Lightly cover with seasoning mix. Gently spread sour cream in a layer over the beans and seasoning, being careful not to mix. Scatter olives in a layer over the sour cream, then a layer of tomatoes, then scallions. Serve immediately.

Lee May's Sardine and Egg Dip

~

MAKES 3/4 CUP / PREPARATION TIME: 10 MINUTES

Dipping isn't always a communal affair. It can also be solitary comfort food. Lee May, the *Atlanta Journal-Constitution*'s gardening columnist, reminded me of this when he told me about a couple of his favorite dips. "You know what potted meat is?" he asked. "I mix it with about a tablespoon of mayonnaise, Tabasco to taste and, when I really get fancy, I put in a little sage or seafood seasoning. I get myself a hunk of cheddar and some soda crackers, and I'm in high cotton."

I know what potted meat is — and that's all I want to know about it. I was more curious about his sardine dip.

1 3.75-ounce tin sardines, drained
1 hard-boiled egg, peeled and chopped
1 to 2 tablespoons mayonnaise or salad dressing
1 tablespoon chopped onion
black pepper and hot pepper sauce to taste
chopped garlic for garnish ("for when I feel really anti-social")

In a small bowl, combine ingredients and mash. Eat immediately.

Dessert Dips

~

No party spread is complete without something sweet. Let the dipping continue through the dessert course! Set out a tray of fruit and perhaps some cubes of ready-made pound cake or angel food cake, along with one — or a selection — of these dips. Most feature flavors associated with more elaborate desserts: tiramisù, pumpkin pie, chocolate truffles, cheesecake. But the preparation in most cases involves little more than melting the ingredients in a fondue pot or whirling them together in a blender. These recipes typically aren't just for dipping — some make refreshing cold soups; others can be served as a sauce over cake, fruit or ice cream.

Caramel-Champagne Dip

For a grown-up version of caramel apples, dip apple slices into this warm, elegant sauce. Bananas, pears and peaches are also suitable for dunking. It's also great over vanilla ice cream.

> 1 1/2 cups sugar
> 2 tablespoons light corn syrup
> 2 tablespoons unsalted butter
> 1 cup heavy cream
> 1/4 cup champagne

In a heavy skillet, over medium-low heat, cook sugar and corn syrup until melted and light golden brown. Stir with a wooden spoon to help dissolve any lumps. Remove skillet from the heat. Slowly add butter and cream, stirring gently and constantly. Add champagne. Return to heat and cook slowly until a slightly thick consistency is reached and a candy thermometer reads 220 degrees. Transfer to a serving bowl. Serve warm.

Vanilla Crème Anglaise

~

MAKES 2 CUPS / PREPARATION TIME: 35 MINUTES
CHILLING TIME: 3 HOURS TO OVERNIGHT

This classic dessert sauce is wonderful for dipping all kinds of fruit, as well as cake, but my favorite way to serve it is to dip small Meringue Spoons (directions follow), then drop a fresh raspberry on top.

2 cups milk
4 egg yolks
1/2 cup sugar
1 tablespoon vanilla

In the bottom of a double boiler, scald milk. Meanwhile, in the top of the double boiler, beat egg yolks and sugar with a wooden spoon until light and fluffy. Remove top of double boiler. Stir the hot milk slowly into the egg mixture. Rinse out the bottom of the pot, add an inch or so of water and assemble the double boiler. Cook and stir the crème until it thickens and coats the back of the spoon. Remove from heat and stir in vanilla. Set aside to cool for about 30 minutes, stirring often to prevent a skin from forming on the top. Cover and refrigerate for 3 hours to overnight.

Meringue Spoons

4 egg whites
1 cup sugar
pinch of salt
pinch of cream of tartar

Preheat oven to 375 degrees. In a medium bowl, with an electric mixer, beat the egg whites until foamy. Slowly add the sugar, then the salt and cream of tartar. Continue beating until stiff peaks form. Line a baking sheet with parchment paper. Put the egg whites into a pastry bag with a 1/4-inch pastry tip and make a 2-inch line with a small loop on the end (shaped like a "P"). Place in the hot oven, then immediately turn off the heat. Leave the meringues in the oven for at least 4 hours, preferably overnight, or until they become dry and crisp. Remove from parchment paper and store in an air-tight container until ready to serve (otherwise they will absorb moisture from the air and lose their crispness).

Espresso Dip

~

MAKES 1 CUP / PREPARATION TIME: 10 MINUTES
CHILLING TIME: AT LEAST 1 HOUR

Chocolate-dipped cherries have become a classic . . . but coffee-dipped cherries? That suggestion comes from the Northwest Cherry Growers, and it's a winner. Fresh cherries, apples, bananas, chocolate wafers, pound cake and toasted ladyfingers would all benefit from a dunk in this.

1/4 cup sugar
1/4 cup hot, brewed espresso
8 ounces cream cheese
1 teaspoon vanilla
chocolate-covered coffee beans for garnish (optional)

Dissolve sugar in hot espresso. In a medium bowl, with an electric mixer, beat cream cheese until light and fluffy. Beat in espresso until thoroughly incorporated. Stir in vanilla. Cover and refrigerate for at least 1 hour. When ready to serve, garnish with coffee beans.

Sherried Lime Dip

~

MAKES ABOUT 1 1/4 CUPS / PREPARATION TIME: 10 MINUTES
CHILLING TIME: 1 HOUR

The bar staple Rose's lime juice has uses beyond mixed drinks. It also makes a refreshing South Floridian dip. Accompany with strawberries, pineapple, carambola (star fruit) or vanilla wafers.

8 ounces cream cheese, softened *1/4 cup Rose's lime juice*
1/4 cup sugar *1/4 cup dry sherry*

In a blender or food processor, combine ingredients and blend until smooth. Transfer to a serving bowl. Refrigerate for 1 hour.

Coconut Dip

~

MAKES ABOUT 2 1/4 CUPS / PREPARATION TIME: 5 MINUTES / CHILLING TIME: 1 HOUR

This tropical-tasting recipe gets the award for the cleverest concoction using only two ingredients. Dip with strawberries, pineapple chunks, peaches, papaya, grapes.

8 ounces cream cheese, softened *1 15-ounce can sweetened cream of coconut*

In a medium bowl, with an electric mixer, beat cream cheese until fluffy. Gradually beat in cream of coconut. Transfer to a serving bowl. Cover and refrigerate for 1 hour.

Melanie and Dan's Wedding Reception Dip

~

MAKES 3 CUPS / PREPARATION TIME: 15 MINUTES
CHILLING TIME: AT LEAST 1 HOUR

At Melanie and Dan Hogan's wedding reception in Marietta, Georgia, guests stuck close to the buffet table, mainly so they could keep dipping into the fluffy, cheesecake-like concoction prepared especially by Melanie's mom, Mary Creasman of Cleveland, Tennessee. She recommends fresh strawberries and sliced peaches for dipping.

8 ounces light cream cheese
1 cup powdered sugar
1 7-ounce jar marshmallow cream
8 ounces light whipped topping
1 teaspoon vanilla
1/2 teaspoon red food coloring (optional)

In a large bowl, with an electric mixer, beat together the cream cheese and powdered sugar until smooth. Blend in the marshmallow cream, whipped topping, vanilla and red food coloring. Transfer to a serving bowl. Cover and refrigerate for at least 1 hour before serving.

Cranberry-Cream Cheese Dip

~

MAKES 1 CUP / PREPARATION TIME: 15 MINUTES
CHILLING TIME: AT LEAST 1 HOUR

Cranberry sauce is good for more than relish, as this pretty dip proves. Serve with apple wedges, pear wedges, pineapple chunks, bananas, grapes.

4 ounces cream cheese, softened
2 tablespoons half-and-half
1/2 cup finely chopped nuts (pecans,
  walnuts or macadamia nuts)
1/2 cup cranberry sauce
raspberries, shredded coconut for garnish (optional)

In a blender, or a medium bowl, beat cream cheese until smooth. Stir in half-and-half, nuts and cranberry sauce. Blend until mixture reaches desired consistency. Transfer to a serving bowl. Garnish with raspberries and coconut. Cover and refrigerate for at least 1 hour.

Toffee Apple Dip

~

MAKES ABOUT 2 1/2 CUPS / PREPARATION TIME: 10 MINUTES

In truth, you can produce a great dip for apples just by mixing brown sugar and a little vanilla with cream cheese. But why not go for pure decadence by adding chopped toffee candy? Tart Granny Smith apples are just the thing to balance the sweetness.

8 ounces cream cheese, softened
1 teaspoon vanilla
1/2 cup sugar
3/4 cup packed brown sugar
1 6-ounce package Bits O' Brickle
(or other toffee candy)

In a medium, microwave-safe bowl, with an electric mixer, blend cream cheese, vanilla, sugar and brown sugar. Stir in Bits O' Brickle. Cook in microwave oven on HIGH for 3 minutes. Stir, then cook for 1 minute more. Serve warm or at room temperature.

Gingered Pumpkin Dip

~

MAKES ABOUT 4 CUPS / PREPARATION TIME: 10 MINUTES
CHILLING TIME: 1 HOUR TO OVERNIGHT

No time to bake a pumpkin pie for Thanksgiving? Whip up this yummy dip, serve it with graham crackers or gingersnaps, and no one will miss the pie.

8 ounces cream cheese, room temperature
1 16-ounce can pumpkin puree
1 cup packed dark brown sugar
2 teaspoons ground cinnamon
1/2 teaspoon ground ginger
1/2 teaspoon ground nutmeg
chopped candied ginger for garnish (optional)

In a large bowl, with an electric mixer, blend together the cream cheese and pumpkin. Blend in remaining ingredients. Cover and refrigerate for at least 1 hour to overnight. Garnish with candied ginger.

Chocolate Truffle Fondue

~

MAKES 1 1/2 CUPS / PREPARATION TIME: 20 MINUTES

Whenever I hear mention of chocolate fondue, I think about the poor guy at a cocktail party who got so carried away dipping strawberries that he didn't even notice he'd dribbled chocolate sauce down the front of his designer tie. Such is the risk you take. But if you're a true chocoholic, it's worth the potential humiliation.

If there's any left, chill it, scoop out little balls with a spoon and roll them in cocoa. Then you'll understand where this fondue gets its name. Strawberries and raspberries are the ultimate dippers, but any other fruit will work, as well as marshmallows, pound cake, miniature cream puff shells, meringues or plain miniature doughnuts.

8 ounces bittersweet Swiss chocolate, preferably Toblerone,
  with or without nuts, broken
1/2 cup heavy cream
2 to 3 tablespoons kirsch, brandy or other liqueur (optional)

In the top of a small double boiler, over simmering water, combine chocolate and cream. Stir until chocolate is melted and mixture is smooth. Stir in liqueur. Set double boiler over fondue flame. (If desired, warm the liqueur first and ignite it, then pour over the chocolate. When flame dies out, stir liqueur in.) Serve immediately.

Peanut Butter Cup Fondue

~

MAKES ABOUT 2 CUPS / PREPARATION TIME: 15 MINUTES

Peanut butter lovers of all ages will be unable to resist this candy-like fondue that is heavenly for dipping banana chunks, apple slices and pound cake cubes.

4 ounces unsweetened baking chocolate
1 cup light cream
1 cup sugar
1/4 cup creamy peanut butter
1 teaspoon vanilla

In a medium saucepan, combine chocolate and cream. Cook over low heat, stirring constantly, until chocolate melts and mixture is smooth. Add sugar and peanut butter. Cook until slightly thickened. Remove from heat. Stir in vanilla. Transfer to fondue pot or chafing dish, or serve warm directly from the saucepan.

Ambrosia Dip

〜

MAKES ABOUT 2 CUPS / PREPARATION TIME: 35 MINUTES
CHILLING TIME: 2 TO 3 HOURS

The taste of this citrusy, custard-like dip reminds me of the classic Southern fruit salad, especially if it's paired with a coconut macaroon and perhaps pineapple and orange sections.

1/2 cup sugar
4 teaspoons cornstarch
1 egg
1 cup pineapple juice
juice and grated zest (colored part of peel)
  of 1 medium orange
juice and grated zest of 1 medium lemon
8 ounces cream cheese

In a medium saucepan, whisk together the sugar, cornstarch and egg until thoroughly combined. Whisk in the juices and zests. Cook and stir over medium heat for about 10 minutes, or until mixture is thick enough to coat a spoon. Let cool completely. In a medium bowl, with an electric mixer, beat the cream cheese until fluffy. Beat in the custard mixture. Cover and refrigerate for 2 to 3 hours before serving.

White Chocolate-Cinnamon Fondue

~

MAKES ABOUT 1 CUP / PREPARATION TIME: 40 MINUTES

Infusing white chocolate with cinnamon gives a surprisingly spicy bite to this decadent dip, which marries well with both fruit and cake.

> 2 cinnamon sticks, cut in half lengthwise,
>   broken into several pieces
> 1 cup heavy cream
> 6 ounces white chocolate, chopped

In a small saucepan, combine half of the cinnamon pieces and the cream. Bring to a boil. Remove from heat, cover and let stand for 15 minutes. Add remaining cinnamon pieces and return pan to a boil. Remove from heat, cover and let stand 15 minutes more. In a fondue pot or a medium bowl, place white chocolate. Return cream to a boil once more. Pour cream through a strainer (to remove cinnamon pieces) over white chocolate. Let stand 2 minutes. Stir until smooth. Serve warm in a fondue pot or small ramekin.

Tiramisù Dip

~

MAKES 3 CUPS / PREPARATION TIME: 15 MINUTES
CHILLING TIME: 1 HOUR

Tiramisù is a signature dessert in Italian restaurants everywhere. Here's how you can recreate those flavors at home with considerably less effort.

> 1 cup sour cream
> 1/4 cup mascarpone cheese
> 1/2 cup packed brown sugar
> 2 tablespoons Marsala wine
> 1 tablespoon strong brewed coffee
> 1 cup heavy cream
> chocolate-covered coffee beans for garnish
>   (optional)

In a food processor or medium bowl, with an electric mixer, combine sour cream, mascarpone cheese, brown sugar, Marsala wine and coffee. Blend well. Cover and refrigerate for 1 hour. In another medium bowl, with an electric mixer, whip the heavy cream to soft peaks, about 5 minutes. When ready to serve, fold whipped cream into the chilled mixture and garnish with chocolate-covered coffee beans.

Chocolate-Hazelnut Dip

~

MAKES 2 1/2 CUPS / PREPARATION TIME: 10 MINUTES
CHILLING TIME: 2 HOURS

Thank God someone finally thought to start selling hazelnuts already peeled of their tight-fitting outer skin. Gourmet markets are your best bet to find them. If they're not in your market, you can peel them yourself — but what a pain! Place them in a single layer in a shallow roasting pan in a 400-degree oven for 10 to 15 minutes. Cool slightly, then rub them between a towel to remove the skins. Fresh pear slices, bananas, or cake cubes could use a coat of this.

1/2 cup skinned hazelnuts
1 1/2 cups heavy cream
8 ounces bittersweet chocolate,
  chopped into large pieces

In a heavy skillet, over low heat, toast the nuts, stirring frequently, until golden brown and fragrant, about 5 minutes. Transfer to a food processor. Pulse until finely chopped. Set aside. In a heavy medium saucepan, bring cream to a low boil. In a medium bowl, place chocolate and immediately cover with cream, stirring until chocolate is melted. Stir in nuts. Transfer mixture to a serving bowl. Cover and refrigerate for 2 hours. Serve cold or warm.

Mango Dip

~

MAKES 2 CUPS / PREPARATION TIME: 10 MINUTES
CHILLING TIME: 1 HOUR

This light dip could also be served as a cold soup with a dollop of sour cream or yogurt, or as a sauce over fresh fruit or pound cake. For a thicker consistency, drain the excess whey from the yogurt; or use yogurt cheese instead (page 57). Peaches or nectarines, incidentally, would work just as well in place of the mango. Serve with strawberries, kiwi, carambola (star fruit), papaya chunks, cantaloupe, honeydew, cherries, vanilla wafers.

1 cup peeled, diced mangoes (fresh or packed in light syrup, drained)
1 cup plain yogurt, drained of excess whey

2 tablespoons packed brown sugar
2 teaspoons lemon juice or lime juice

In a blender, combine ingredients. Blend until smooth. Cover and refrigerate for 1 hour.

Banana-Butterscotch Dip

~

MAKES 3 CUPS / PREPARATION TIME: 15 MINUTES / CHILLING TIME: 1 HOUR

This flavor duo works well with banana slices, cake slices, apple slices.

1/2 cup butterscotch morsels
1 1/2 cups banana nectar (such as Loóza brand)

2 ripe bananas, sliced
4 ounces cream cheese

In a medium saucepan, over low heat, combine butterscotch morsels and banana nectar. Slowly bring to a low boil, stirring morsels until they melt and blend with the juice. Transfer mixture to a food processor or blender. Add bananas and cream cheese. Process until well blended. Transfer mixture to a serving bowl. Cover and refrigerate for 1 hour.

Caribbean Eggnog Dip

MAKES 3 CUPS / PREPARATION TIME: 30 MINUTES
CHILLING TIME: 4 HOURS TO OVERNIGHT

Mary Louise Lever of Rome, Georgia, has a knack for winning cooking contests like no one we've ever met. She's received top honors in more than 50 contests — most recently, the $25,000 grand prize in the National Chicken Cooking Contest. Like her mother, Bessie Burk (whose recipe for Baked Fiesta Spinach Dip is on page 25), she knows what will grab a judge's attention: an intriguing twist, easy-to-follow directions and a delicious-sounding name. This fluffy, festive dip is a perfect example. Serve it with pineapple chunks, strawberries, carambola (star fruit) slices and gingersnaps.

1 1/2 cups dairy eggnog
2 tablespoons cornstarch
1 teaspoon grated fresh ginger
1/2 cup whipping cream
1 tablespoon sugar

1/2 cup sour cream
1 tablespoon light rum or 1 teaspoon
* pure rum extract*
freshly grated nutmeg for garnish
* (optional)*

In a saucepan, combine eggnog, cornstarch and ginger. Cook and stir over medium heat until thickened and it begins to bubble. Cook 2 minutes more. Remove from heat and cover with plastic wrap. Let cool. In a large bowl, whip cream and sugar until stiff peaks form. Fold in sour cream, rum and eggnog mixture. Cover and refrigerate for at least 4 hours to overnight. Garnish with grated nutmeg. When serving, keep cold in a crushed ice-lined bowl.

Brie and Strawberry Spread

~

MAKES 1 8-INCH BRIE WHEEL / PREPARATION TIME: 5 MINUTES

When I am in need of an instant dessert, especially one to take to an outdoor gathering, I fall back on this one that Iris Broudy, former food editor for the *Cleveland Plain Dealer*, taught me. Let it soften to room temperature, then spread on gingersnaps.

> *1 8-inch brie wheel*
> *About 1/2 of a 6-ounce package strawberry cream cheese spread*
> *(or other fruit-flavored cream cheese)*

Frost the brie wheel with enough cream cheese spread to cover thickly. When ready to serve, bring to room temperature.

Acknowledgments

I am grateful to my husband, Jim Smith, who not only helped in the tasting, but also in the less tasty tasks of proofreading, copyediting and indexing into the wee hours of the morning. My mother, Nancy Puckett, shopped, tested recipes, organized tastings and kept our lives sane. Al and Mary Ann Clayton brought the recipes to life with their expert food styling and photography; Mary Ann also developed many of the dips and dippers that were chosen for the book. Kristin Eddy, Margaret Ann Surber, David Cleveland, Vicky Murphy, Lenada Merrick, Kitty Crider, Kathleen Purvis and Elizabeth Lee were invaluable in developing, testing and researching recipes, as was Pam Auchmutey, who also lent her editing talents. Thanks to Mara Reid Rogers for sharing her great recipes and presentation ideas; to my sister Patti Puckett for her research help; to Tony Conway and Jill Wendholt Silva for their recipe leads; to the folks at Kraft and Lipton for providing background material; and to Jim Auchmutey for his writing advice.

I especially appreciate the support and encouragement from my editors at the *Atlanta Journal-Constitution*, Lea Donosky and Susan Soper.

And finally, thanks to Jill Dible for the care and creativity she put into the book's design, and to John Yow, Chuck Perry and the other folks at Longstreet for making the project happen.

Here are a few of the books that I found particularly useful for background:

Entertaining by Martha Stewart (Clarkson Potter, 1982)
Fashionable Food by Sylvia Lovegren (Macmillan, 1995)
Party Food by Barbara Kafka (Morrow, 1992)
Populuxe by Thomas Hine (Alfred A. Knopf, 1987)
Square Meals by Jane and Michael Stern (Knopf, 1984)

Other Recipe Contributors

Thanks to the following cooks, professional and nonprofessional,
who provided recipes or inspiration for recipes:

Kay Baker (Polynesian Ginger Dip)
Gwen Bradley (Chutney Yogurt Dip)
Anne Byrn (Good Luck Dip, White Chocolate-
  Cinnamon Fondue)
Evelyn Camp (Curried Bacon-Peanut Dip, Sweet
  Mustard Dip)
Julie Barkin Carlyle (Asparagus and Tuna Mousse)
Garnet Carr (Smoked Oyster Dip)
Lisa Clark (Politically Correct Mushroom Pâté)
Elaine Commins (Fresh Lemon-Basil Dip)
René Cottrell (Pesto, Salmon and Cream Cheese
  Loaf)
Catherine Crawford (New Jersey Hot Crab Dip)
Joan Demer (Hot Broccoli-Almond Dip, Onion-
  Caper Dip)
Helen Dollaghan (Tarragon-Chicken Pâté)
Louise Doyle (Blue Hawaii Dip)
Mrs. D. E. Evans (Brandied Blue Cheese Spread)
Amy Fischer (Easy Black Bean and Corn Dip)
Marilyn Fox (Spicy Beet and Horseradish Dip)
Brianna Hadquist (Sherried Lime Dip)
Carol Horstman (Liptauer Cheese Spread)
Packy Johnson (Blender Salad Dip)
Ruth A. Jones (Hot-cha-cha Black Bean Dip)
Betty Kinman (Confetti Dip)
Jack Kirkpatrick (Holiday Ham Dip)
Kim Kubach (Hot Honey Hummus Dip)
Del Martin (Vampire Vaccine, Tomato-Feta Dip)
Marla Martin (Toffee Apple Dip)

Liz McKelvey (Niçoise Dip)
Virginia Miller (Ricotta-Pesto Mousse)
Sandy Overton (Curried Chutney Dip)
Claire Peeler (Cranberry-Cream Cheese Dip)
Sandy Reese (Sombrero Spread)
Billie Rickman (Coconut Dip)
Mara Reid Rogers (Creamy Lemon-Dill Dip,
  Homemade Boursin With Scallions and Parsley)
Alice W. Rylander (Low Country Shrimp Paste)
Madeleine D. St. Romain (Gingered Pumpkin Dip)
Judy Schultz (Beer-Cheese Fondue)
Donna Seaman (Reuben Dip)
Becca Simon (Pepperoni Pizza Dip)
Kathy Smith (Better-Than-Ranch Buttermilk Dip)
Gary Solander (Jalapeño Jelly Dip)
Sondra Visner (Chopped Green Bean Pâté)
Anne Waldrop (Carrot-Raisin Dip)

Index

Page numbers in italics are photos

Susan Puckett is the award-winning food editor of the *Atlanta Journal-Constitution*. She is the author of *A Cook's Tour of Mississippi* and *A Cook's Tour of Iowa* and the coauthor of *The Ultimate Barbecue Sauce Cookbook*.